WHAT IS SALVATION?

A Biblical Study of God's Greatest Gift

BILL PARKER

ISBN: 978-1-4834-0798-2 (sc)
ISBN: 978-1-4834-0797-5 (e)

Lulu Publishing Services rev. date: 02/19/2014

FOREWORD

This study of the Bible's teaching on the subject of salvation began as a simple revision of an earlier pamphlet with the same title, *What is Salvation?*. In the original pamphlet I considered only one aspect of salvation, the new birth. I decided to do a more extensive study on the subject, dealing with all facets of salvation as taught in the Bible. I have done this for two reasons. The first reason has to do with divisions that have developed in recent years among Gospel churches. As we know from Scripture, whenever divisions occur within churches where the true Gospel is preached consistently and without compromise, it always reveals one of two things about those involved. It either exposes false professors of the truth and reveals true believers as the Apostle Paul expressed – *"For there must be also heresies among you, that they which are approved may be made manifest among you," (1 Corinthians 11:19)*; or it will expose the immaturity, ignorance, and/or remaining sinfulness of true believers as expressed by Paul in another place – *"And I, brethren, could not speak unto you as unto spiritual, but as unto carnal, even as unto babes in Christ. I have fed you with milk, and not with meat: for hitherto ye were not able to bear it, neither yet now are ye able. For ye are yet carnal: for whereas there is among you envying, and strife, and divisions, are ye not carnal, and walk as men?" (1 Corinthians 3:1-3)*.

The second reason is that as I began to study the subject, I was reminded, not only of my own former ignorance of the subject while I myself was in false Christianity but of the fact that many, if not most, so-called Christians are also ignorant of the Bible's teaching on this most important of all subjects – the salvation of sinners by God's free and sovereign grace in the Lord Jesus Christ. It is my desire that as you read these pages you will strive to make it an exercise in self-examination and test yourself and your profession of faith in the Lord Jesus Christ by the standard of the Scriptures alone. You will find that in these pages there is some repetition of words, phrases, ideas, and Scriptural references. It is intentional for the purpose of emphasis. As you read these pages and study the Bible, may the Lord God reveal Himself in your hearts. All Scriptural references are from the Authorized KJV and printed in bold italics.

William W. (Bill) Parker

ACKNOWLEDGMENTS

While the content for *What is Salvation?* was derived from a series of messages I preached at Thirteenth Street Baptist Church in Ashland, Kentucky, the idea for this publication sprang from the desire to have a written document to complement the video production on this subject. The videos that were produced are presented by me in a teaching series for airing over an eight week period on the weekly 30 minute television program, *Reign of Grace*. This written version of *What is Salvation?* is more detailed and contains additional scripture references; however, these two formats are well suited for use together with the eight segments of the video production of *What is Salvation?* corresponding to the eight chapters of this book.

These professionally produced videos are offered in an attractively packaged, eight DVD set through Reign of Grace Media Ministries, a ministry of Eager Avenue Grace Church of Albany, GA. I wish to acknowledge and thank the members of Eager Avenue Grace Church for their collaboration and support in the production of both formats of *What is Salvation?* Together, they provide excellent source materials for Bible study groups and for any who seriously desire to engage in a comprehensive study of the teachings from God's Word on this vital subject of eternal significance.

As a reflection of this ministry's interest and zeal in promoting God's Gospel, currently this video series is offered free of charge through www.rofgrace.com or by contacting:

Reign of Grace Media Ministries
A Ministry of Eager Avenue Grace Church
1102 Eager Drive
Albany, Georgia 31707-3858
www.rofgrace.com

While I do not pretend to have all the answers, I am convinced that God has provided them in His Word. So first and foremost, I thank Him for His marvelous grace in opening the eyes, ears, and hearts of those He saves so as to behold His glory in their very salvation, God's greatest gift. To God be the glory!

Pastor William W. (Bill) Parker

CONTENTS

CHAPTER

1

INTRODUCTION

The purpose for this series of studies is to explore the truth of salvation as revealed, defined, and taught in the Bible. Salvation is the main subject of the Bible. It includes everything God does FOR His people and IN His people in and by the Lord Jesus Christ. It also includes everything God freely gives His people in the way of eternal, spiritual life and glory. If we are truly saved, the Bible teaches that this salvation includes all that we are, all that we have, and all that we do as we live our lives by the grace and power of God and for the glory of God in the Lord Jesus Christ. In its simplest meaning, the word *salvation* means to be rescued from a dangerous or threatening situation. In the Bible it means both a sinner's ultimate redemption from sin and all consequences of sin. It also means a sinner's reconciliation to God. Salvation in the Bible is deliverance from the ultimate tragedy – the judgment and wrath of God which ends in eternal death and damnation.

The Bible teaches that because of sin the world of fallen men and women deserves and will experience the just and ultimate wrath of God – *"For the wages of sin is death" (Romans 6:23a)*. It also teaches that salvation can only be accomplished by the Lord Jesus Christ Who delivers God's people, all whom He loves, from the wrath to come – *"but the gift of God is eternal life through Jesus Christ our Lord" (Romans 6:23b)*.

It is sad and even tragic that so many people today claim to be saved but really have no idea of the reality of salvation as taught in God's Word. Some people think of salvation as simply believing, but they really do not know or understand what they are required to believe. Others add things such as repentance, obedience, or even making a public profession, being baptized, and joining a church. To others salvation means turning over a new leaf or going through a real moral reformation of life. People often speak of "getting saved." They ask questions like, "When did I (or you) get saved?" Many speak of salvation in other terms like "accepting Jesus as your personal Savior," or "inviting Jesus into your heart." They do not consider that these statements are NOT in the Bible. In fact, there is not anything like them in the Bible. This has led many people to think wrongly that salvation is a one-time event in their lives – something that happened in childhood or youth when they "invited Jesus into their hearts," or "gave their hearts to Jesus."

In the New Testament, the verb *"to save"* (σῴζω – pronounced sō'-zō) appears virtually in every possible tense of the Greek language. Consider the following examples:

THE PAST TENSE OF SALVATION

The past tense of salvation involves matters of both eternity and time. Eternally speaking, there is a sense in which those who are saved have always been saved from the foundation of the world in the eternal mind and purpose of God. This is difficult for us to grasp because we are so limited in our understanding of time, but God is eternal and immutable. Salvation in eternity is expressed by the Apostle Paul in his second epistle to Timothy when he wrote of the power of God *"Who hath saved us, and called us with an holy calling, not according to our works, but according to His own purpose and grace, which was GIVEN US IN CHRIST JESUS BEFORE THE WORLD BEGAN," (2 Timothy 1:9).* Jesus Christ, the second Person of the Holy Trinity, was appointed to be Surety of His people, having the debt of all their sins imputed (charged, accounted) to Him by the Father Who imputed righteousness which Christ Himself would establish in time. The righteousness Christ established is the only ground of salvation for the people of God. Jesus Christ established this righteousness by His death on the cross as the sin-bearing Substitute of God's elect and under His covenant obligation as the Surety of His people.

Hebrews 2 – (16) For verily He took not on Him the nature of angels; but He took on him the seed of Abraham. (17) Wherefore in all things it behoved Him to be made like unto His brethren, that He might be a merciful and faithful high priest in things pertaining to God, to make reconciliation for the sins of the people.

The *"seed of Abraham"* are God's elect out of every nation. They are all whom the Father gave to Christ before the foundation of the world *(cf. John 6:37-40; 17:1-4)*. They are the spiritual *"seed of Abraham"* known by their submission to and faith in the Lord Jesus Christ for all salvation *(cf. Galatians 3:26-29)*. *"Behoved"* is the Greek word for *debt* *(ὀφείλω – pronounced o-fā'-lō)* which describes how Christ obligated Himself under the covenant agreement to stand as Surety for His people. He voluntarily took upon Himself the legal obligation to pay their debt to God's justice. Therefore He had to be *"made flesh" (John 1:14)* without sin and die for their sins imputed to Him.

The past tense of salvation is also expressed in the Bible in referring to the redemption of God's people by the Lord Jesus Christ which took place in time on the cross – *"For by grace are ye saved* (lit. have been saved) *through faith; and that not of yourselves: it is the gift of God: not of works, lest any man should boast" (Ephesians 2:8-9)*. All who are saved were saved at the cross of Calvary when Jesus Christ died for them as their Substitute and Surety, paying the full penalty for all their sins. The righteousness God imputed to His people had to be established in time by Christ on the cross. This great event was future for all the Old Testament saints, but it is past for all New Testament saints.

Another facet of the past tense of salvation has to do with the saved sinner's experience in the new birth. This is the invincible calling of the Holy Spirit through the preaching of the Gospel of God's grace in Christ Jesus whereby God's people are given spiritual life and brought to faith in the Lord Jesus Christ for the first time in their lives. When the Bible tells us in Scriptures such as ***Romans 10:13 – "For whosoever shall call upon the name of the Lord shall be saved,"*** it speaks of a sinner who has been born again by the Holy Spirit calling out of his need upon the Lord for salvation. The indication is clearly that those who have called upon *"the name of the Lord"* are saved when they do so. Therefore, all who are born again by the Holy Spirit and who have called upon *"the name of the Lord"* can say, "We have been saved."

THE PRESENT TENSE OF SALVATION

The present tense of salvation speaks of the continual power and grace of God to preserve all who have been saved and to cause them to persevere in the faith. In this sense, all who are saved can say, "We are BEING saved." This is expressed in Scriptures such as *1 Corinthians 1:18 – "For the preaching of the cross is to them that perish* [lit., who are perishing] *foolishness; but unto us which are saved* [lit., are being saved] *it is the power of God."* Salvation, then, is the continual process of God's power and grace in Christ to bring sinners to final glory in heaven – *"Now unto Him that is able to keep you from falling, and to present you faultless before the presence of His glory with exceeding joy, to the only wise God our Saviour, be glory and majesty, dominion and power, both now and ever. Amen." (Jude 24-25)*

THE FUTURE TENSE OF SALVATION

The future tense of salvation refers to the believer's final glorification in heaven. This will take place when all the saved are glorified in the consummation of all things at the second coming of Christ. The Apostle Paul wrote much of this in *1 Corinthians 15* and *Philippians 3* when he wrote of the resurrection of the dead in Christ. The future tense of salvation is expressed in Scriptures such as ***Romans 13:11 – "And that, knowing the time, that now it is high time to awake out of sleep: for now is our salvation nearer than when we believed."***

As we study salvation revealed and defined in the Bible, keep in mind that there is only one salvation and one way of salvation. What

God has purposed and planned in the past for His people, is worked out by Him in the present, and will be brought to its consummation in the future. Together it is all one salvation. So salvation involves all of these workings of the Lord in eternity and time. But as to a person's experience of salvation, the Bible tells us, *"Believe on the Lord Jesus Christ, and you shall be saved,"* and, *"Whosoever shall CALL upon the name of the Lord shall be saved" (Acts 16:31; Romans 10:13).* But what does it really mean to believe on the Lord Jesus Christ or to call upon His name?

THE NAME "JESUS" MEANS SALVATION

The first time the word *salvation* is used in Scripture is found in **Genesis 49:18** where Jacob in blessing his sons says, *"I have waited for thy salvation, O LORD."* The word *"salvation"* in this verse is the Hebrew word *yesh·ü·'·ä* from which the name Jesus *(Greek - Ἰησοῦς)* is derived. It means *savior, salvation,* or *deliverance.* As recorded in **Matthew 1:21**, when the angel appeared to Joseph concerning Mary, the angel said, *"And she shall bring forth a son, and thou shalt call His name JESUS: for He shall save His people from their sins."* Later, when a man named Simeon saw the baby Jesus, he took the babe in his arms and said, *"Lord, now lettest thou thy servant depart in peace, according to thy word: For mine eyes have seen Thy salvation," (Luke 2:29-30)*, or the salvation God freely provides for His people in the Lord Jesus Christ. To believe on the Lord Jesus Christ, or to call upon His name, therefore, is to believe God's testimony concerning Him in the doctrine of Scripture. So what exactly are we commanded by God to believe?

If we are to consider the matter of salvation biblically, we must first ask ourselves, "Do we have the TRUE Gospel?" The Bible tells us the Gospel of Christ *"is the power of God unto salvation to every one that believeth; to the Jew first, and also to the Greek. For therein is the righteousness of God revealed from faith to faith: as it is written, The just shall live by faith." (Romans 1:16-17)* The Lord Jesus Himself said, *"Repent ye, and believe the Gospel." (Mark 1:15)* The Bible tells us that there are false gospels leading to eternal death. So we must get the Gospel right. What comes in the name of Christianity today has reduced the Gospel to formulas like the four spiritual laws, or a set of questions people ask, and if a person answers "yes" to the questions and prays a prayer, they tell that person, "You are saved." All this does is create false Christians with false hope and assurance. There is nothing biblical about this kind of method under a false gospel.

Many today quote *John 3:16* as the Gospel and conclude from that one verse that the Gospel is "God loves you, and Christ died for you." But that is not the Gospel! The true Gospel is not "God loves everybody, and Christ died for everybody, therefore, it is your decision either to accept Him or reject Him." First of all, that makes salvation conditioned on the sinner and not on Christ, the Savior. Secondly, why would one sinner believe in or accept Jesus as his/her personal savior, and another sinner not believe in or accept Him? Is it because the one who believes is a better person than one who refuses to believe? Is the one who believes less stubborn, less obstinate, and less rebellious? The Bible tells us this is not the case.

The Bible clearly teaches that man by nature will not of his own will seek or believe in Jesus Christ for all salvation. It sets forth in passages such as *Romans 3:9-20*, which we will consider later, the universal and total depravity of all men. Total depravity does not teach that we all as sinful men and women are as bad as we could be, but it does teach that all of us have been so affected by sin in every part of our being (our minds, affections, wills – our hearts) that we cannot produce a righteousness that will satisfy the perfection required by the holy law of God. Total depravity also means we are so spiritually dead in trespasses and sin that we by nature (as we are born naturally in the flesh) have no desire to seek after or choose God and His way of salvation in and by Jesus Christ.

Total depravity and the need for salvation go all the way back to man's fall from favor and loss of communion with God that took place when Adam first sinned as recorded in the third chapter of *Genesis*. Since the fall of all mankind in Adam, the life of all men and women has been marked by sin and death. When Adam disobeyed God, he did so, not merely as a private person, but as the representative of the whole human race. If we are to learn to think biblically concerning salvation, we must learn to think biblically about our fall in Adam, our sin, and need of salvation. When Adam sinned, we all sinned, not personally but in Adam as our representative –

Romans 5 – (12) Wherefore, as by one man sin entered into the world, and death by sin; and so death passed upon all men, for that all have sinned:

This verse literally says that *"all sinned"* in Adam. We will deal more with this later. The Bible also tells us that *"all have sinned, and come short of the glory of God" (Romans 3:23)* and that *"the wages of sin is death" (Romans 6:23a)*. This is the case for all of us without exception unless a way of salvation can be found. Thank God that the Bible shows how a way, the one and only way, of salvation has been found – *"but the gift of God is eternal life through Jesus Christ our Lord" (Romans 6:23b)*. Let's consider *John 3:16-17*

John 3 – (16) For God so loved the world, that He gave His only begotten Son, that whosoever believeth in Him should not perish, but have everlasting life. (17) For God sent not His Son into the world to condemn the world; but that the world through Him might be saved.

The *"world"* in *John 3:16* is the world of God's chosen people IN CHRIST who come to believe in Him. Salvation is not procured and settled by their believing but by the death of Christ as written in *John 3:14-15* –

John 3 – (14) And as Moses lifted up the serpent in the wilderness, even so must the Son of man be lifted up: (15) That whosoever believeth in Him should not perish, but have eternal life.

This speaks of Christ's death on the cross for the sins of His people. Jesus Christ is said in the Bible to be *"the Savior of the world" (John 4:42; 1 John 4:14)*, not because He is trying to save everyone without exception, but because He is the Savior of all who are saved without distinction, Jew and Gentile. In the Bible, the *world* never means all without exception. An example of this is found in *1 John 5:19 – "And we know that we are of God, and the whole world lieth in wickedness."* Hardly anyone would argue that *"the whole world"* here means all without exception. The Gospel does not tell all without exception that God loves them and Christ died for them. It does, however, tell all who hear its message that God's love is proven and expressed in that He sent His Son into the world to die for His people and that God's love can only be found and experienced in the Lord Jesus Christ – *"He that believeth on the Son hath everlasting life: and he that believeth not the Son shall not see life; but the wrath of God abideth on him" (John 3:36).* So we must first make sure that we know and believe the true Gospel. To see this more clearly, let's begin by stating:

FOUR VITAL TRUTHS ABOUT SALVATION

(1) Salvation is salvation from sin. The reason we need salvation is because mankind has been ruined by the fall. Death, hell, and the wrath of God are all the consequences and just penalties of sin. As we saw before, *"the wages of sin is death."* Paul wrote in *1 Corinthians 15:56 – "The sting of death is sin; and the strength of sin is the law."* The *"law"* encompasses all the commandments and revealed will of God concerning our character, conduct, even our thoughts. The perfect and just law of God must pronounce the sentence of death where there is any breach of the law, where sin is found and rightfully charged or imputed. The mandate of God's law is simply "do and live;" the penalty of God's holy law is simply "disobey and die."

When the Bible speaks of Jesus Christ as Savior, it conveys the truth that He saves His people from sin. As we stated before, the angel told Joseph concerning Mary's child -- *And she shall bring forth a son, and thou shalt call His name JESUS: for He shall save His people from their sins." (Matthew 1:21)* It is so important to realize that we all need salvation from sin. We all need to be redeemed from sin. Sin separates man from God, and God has emphatically declared that sin, if not miraculously, powerfully, and justly removed, will end in death *(cf. James 1:14).*

(2) **Salvation must be established upon righteousness**. If you have never thought about or considered the following issue, then you have not heard or believed the true Gospel of salvation as revealed in the Bible. The greatest problem presented in the Bible is this – **If God is just, how can He forgive sin?** The moment anyone says, "God saves sinners," or "God forgives sin," there is a great theological, legal, and ethical problem that cannot be solved by man. None of the major or minor religions of man have been able to solve this problem or even come close to solving it. Think about this! If God is holy, just, good, and righteous, He cannot forgive sin any more than a human judge can justly set a proven, convicted murderer free by simply saying, "I forgive you, go free." On the other hand, if I were to say God sentences all sinners to eternal damnation and death, there would be no problem. This would be a matter of God simply giving us as sinners what we deserve and what we have earned. This is what God's justice demands. The problem arises when we speak of salvation for sinners. The fact is this – God is holy, righteous, just, and true. GOD MUST BE JUST IN ALL THAT HE DOES! In the matter of salvation, which is a marvelous act of God's love, grace, and mercy, God cannot ignore, deny, or even compromise His justice – His righteousness – else He would cease to be God. So if God forgives sinners; if God saves sinners, He must do it in a way so as to honor His holy law and inflexible justice. He must do it in a righteous way, and righteousness by definition is perfect satisfaction to God's law and justice. God, therefore, must be, as recorded by the prophet Isaiah in *Isaiah 45:21* – *"A JUST GOD AND SAVIOR."*

Salvation from sin, therefore, can only be attained and maintained based on perfect righteousness – perfect obedience and perfect satisfaction to God's justice. This is the reason that no righteousness of sinful man will do. First of all, men by nature have no righteousness before God. Secondly, because we are born spiritually dead, i.e., dead in trespasses and sin, and because we are sinners, we cannot produce the righteousness required by God's holy law. In fact the Bible tells us that the best efforts of sinful man to produce righteousness always fail. Consider God's description of fallen men and women by nature. In the first part of the *Book of Romans*, the Apostle Paul proved how both Jew and Gentile were sinners and deserved eternal death and damnation. He wrote,

Romans 3 – (9) What then? are we better than they? No, in no wise: for we have before proved both Jews and Gentiles, that they are all under sin; (10) As it is written, There is none righteous, no, not one: (11) There is none that understandeth, there is none that seeketh after God. (12) They are all gone out of the way, they are together become unprofitable; there is none that doeth good, no, not one. (13) Their throat is an open sepulchre; with their tongues they have used deceit; the poison of asps is under their lips: (14) Whose mouth is full of cursing and bitterness: (15) Their feet are swift to shed blood: (16) Destruction and misery are in their ways: (17) And the way of peace have they not known: (18) There is no fear of God before their eyes.

The law of God, therefore, can only pronounce a sinner to be guilty, and such guilt renders that sinner helpless to be saved by his/her attempts to keep the law –

Romans 3 – (19) Now we know that what things soever the law saith, it saith to them who are under the law: that every mouth may be stopped, and all the world may become guilty before God. (20) Therefore by the deeds of the law there shall no flesh be justified in his sight: for by the law is the knowledge of sin.

The law can only expose a sinner, even at his/her best, to be sinful and justly deserving of death. Whenever sinful men and women seek to be righteous before God by their works so as to gain or maintain salvation, they are rejected. Why? It is because God is holy and just, and the best works of the best of men do not equal perfect righteousness. Such efforts are acts of pride, self-righteousness, and unbelief. The Apostle Paul wrote in *Galatians 2:21 – I do not frustrate the grace of God: for if righteousness come by the law, then Christ is dead in vain.* Sinners who seek to be saved by their works and efforts to keep the law deny the glory, necessity, and power of Jesus Christ in His death to establish righteousness for His people. The issues in salvation, then, have to do with the following:

First, how can sinful man be justified before a holy God? *(cf. Job 9:2)*

Secondly, how can a holy and just God save sinners and remain true to Himself? Or to state it another way, **how can God be just and still justify the ungodly?** *(cf. Isaiah 45:21)*

Consider what it means to be justified. It means: **(a) to be cleared of all the guilt of sin;** and **(b) to be actually counted, or declared, righteous in God's sight.** How can this be in the case of sinners? It is certainly not by works of righteousness which we do, have done, or will do. Where can we as sinners find righteousness or a way to become righteous before holy God? These are the questions with which all sinners need to be confronted in the matter of salvation. Why? It is because God requires perfection. Some may argue it is unfair and unjust for God to require perfection from us. The truth is that God can do no less because He is holy. It cannot be considered unfair when God has freely provided the only way of salvation based on righteousness. The third truth about biblical salvation answers this problem.

(3) Salvation is totally by God's grace, all in and by the Lord Jesus Christ. The only way for sinful men and women to be saved is by redemption through the blood of Jesus Christ. The Bible teaches that Jesus Christ, the Son of God, is the one and only Savior from sin –

Romans 5 – (18) Therefore as by the offence of one [Adam] *judgment came upon all men to condemnation; even so by the righteousness of one* [Jesus Christ] *the free gift came upon all men unto justification of life. (19) For as by one man's* [Adam's] *disobedience many were made sinners, so by the obedience of one* [Jesus Christ] *shall many be made righteous.*

All whom Adam represented in the garden (the whole human family) fell into sin and death when Adam fell. All whom Jesus Christ represented on the cross (the whole election of grace) were justified in and by Him and based on the righteousness HE alone produced by His obedience unto death. Salvation is all of grace, but be assured that grace must be founded upon righteousness –

Romans 5 – (21) That as sin hath reigned unto death, even so might grace reign through righteousness unto eternal life by Jesus Christ our Lord.

The Bible reveals and presents salvation as conditioned on the Lord Jesus Christ, NOT on sinners. The success of salvation is dependent upon two realities – **(a) the glorious person of Jesus Christ (who He is); and (b) the finished work of Jesus Christ (what He accomplished in His death).** Consider first THE PERSON OF JESUS CHRIST. The Apostle Paul wrote that the Gospel concerns God's Son *"Jesus Christ our Lord, which was made of the seed of David according to the flesh; And declared to be the Son of God with power, according to the spirit of holiness, by the resurrection from the dead:" (Romans 1:3-4).* Recall how that when the angel revealed to Joseph that Mary's child would be named *"JESUS,"* because *He shall save His people from their sins (Matthew 1:21)*, there was another name revealed showing the deity of Jesus Christ – *"Behold, a virgin shall be with child, and shall bring forth a son, and they shall call His name Emmanuel, which being interpreted is, God with us" (Matthew 1:23).*

The Apostle John wrote of Christ as the Word of God – *"In the beginning was the Word, and the Word was with God, and the Word was God" (John 1:1)*; He went on to write, *"And the Word was made flesh, and dwelt among us, (and we beheld his glory, the glory as of the only begotten of the Father,) full of grace and truth" (John 1:14).* JESUS CHRIST IS GOD AND MAN IN ONE PERSON – *"Great is the mystery of godliness: God was manifest in the flesh," (1 Timothy 3:16).* Jesus Christ had to be both God and man without sin for Him to be able to save His people from sin. Man cannot create, give, or sustain life, but this Person who is man is able to do this. God cannot die, but this Person who is God did die. As Godman Jesus Christ was made personally responsible (accountable) to keep the law of God and satisfy the justice of God through His obedience unto death acting in the place of His people as SUBSTITUTE and SURETY. This is the debt of the sins of His people imputed to Him.

Hebrews 2 – (14) Forasmuch then as the children [God's elect] *are partakers of flesh and blood, He* [Jesus Christ] *also Himself likewise took part of the same; that through death He might destroy him that had the power of death, that is, the devil; (15) And deliver them who through fear of death were all their lifetime subject to bondage. (16) For verily He took not on Him the nature of angels; but He took on Him the seed of Abraham* [God's elect]. *(17) Wherefore in all things it behoved* [Greek word for *debt*] *Him to be made like unto His brethren* [God's elect], *that He might be a merciful and faithful high priest in things pertaining to God, to make reconciliation for the sins of the people* [God's elect] *(18) For in that He Himself hath suffered being tempted, He is able to succour them that are tempted.*

Consider next THE FINISHED WORK OF JESUS CHRIST. All true preachers of the true Gospel want to preach and talk about God's love to His people. The true Gospel teaches us that in Jesus Christ God's love freely provided what His justice demanded, which is righteousness. The Apostle John wrote – *"… having loved His own which were in the world, He loved them unto the end" (John 13:1).* The *"end"* is the finishing of the work He was given to do. When Jesus Christ did His great work on the cross, He cried, *"It is finished" (John 19:30).* What was *"finished,"* meaning perfected and completed? He accomplished the full and final redemption of His people, the ground of forgiveness for all their sins. Righteousness was *"finished,"* and this is *"the righteousness of God revealed"* in the Gospel *(cf. Romans 1:16-17).* This phrase, *"THE RIGHTEOUSNESS OF GOD,"* is one of the most important phrases in the entire Bible, because it reveals both the person and work of the Lord Jesus Christ as the one and only ground of salvation. It is the entire merit, value, and excellence of the obedience unto death of the Lord Jesus Christ for His people.

This *"righteousness of God"* has been freely imputed (charged, accounted) to everyone of God's elect so that they all are, as the Apostle

Paul wrote, *"justified freely by His grace through the redemption that is in Christ Jesus: Whom God hath set forth to be a propitiation through faith in His blood, to declare His righteousness for the remission of sins that are past, through the forbearance of God; To declare, I say, at this time His righteousness: that He might be just, and the justifier of him which believeth in Jesus" (Romans 3:24-26).* The Apostle Paul explained this by expounding the words of King David from *Psalm 32* – *"Even as David also describeth the blessedness of the man, unto whom God imputeth righteousness without works, Saying, Blessed are they whose iniquities are forgiven, and whose sins are covered. Blessed is the man to whom the Lord will not impute sin" (Romans 4:6-8).*

In salvation, God does not impute sin to His people because He has already imputed their sins to Christ – *"God was in Christ, reconciling the world unto Himself, not imputing their trespasses unto them; and hath committed unto us the word of reconciliation. Now then we are ambassadors for Christ, as though God did beseech you by us: we pray you in Christ's stead, be ye reconciled to God. For He hath made Him to be sin for us, Who knew no sin; that we might be made the righteousness of God in Him" (2 Corinthians 5:19-21).* Consider the prophecy of Isaiah in *Isaiah 53:11* – *"He shall see of the travail of His soul, and shall be satisfied: by His knowledge shall my righteous servant justify many; for He shall bear their iniquities."*

Someone may ask, "What about faith in salvation?" The Bible teaches that where righteousness has been imputed, faith is given to receive and submit to Christ as our whole righteousness before God –

Romans 10 – (4) For Christ is the end of the law for righteousness to every one that believeth.

As to a sinner's personal experience of salvation, when he is born again by the Holy Spirit under the preaching of the Gospel, when the Holy Spirit imparts spiritual life and gives him faith, he believes, receives, rests in, and lays hold of Christ. He submits to Christ as his only righteousness before God. His heart, his conscience is cleansed from the guilt of sin realizing that he is righteous before God in the Lord

Jesus Christ. This is when a sinner is brought to repentance as described by the Apostle Paul –

Philippians 3 – (7) But what things were gain to me, those I counted loss for Christ. (8) Yea doubtless, and I count all things but loss for the excellency of the knowledge of Christ Jesus my Lord: for Whom I have suffered the loss of all things, and do count them but dung, that I may win Christ, (9) And be found in Him, not having mine own righteousness, which is of the law, but that which is through the faith of Christ, the righteousness which is of God by faith:

(4) Salvation is of the Lord, **not of man.** Salvation is NOT a matter of "God has done all He can do, now the rest is up to you." It is all of God, all by His grace, all conditioned on and fulfilled by the Lord Jesus Christ –

Ephesians 2 – (8) For by grace are ye saved through faith; and that not of yourselves: it is the gift of God: (9) Not of works, lest any man should boast.

Salvation is not a human work, and it is not based on, empowered or secured by the works or the wills of sinful men. Sinful human beings cannot save themselves and by nature do not want salvation God's way. Salvation is totally a divine work. It is both OF THE LORD and FROM THE LORD. Even the new birth is totally of the Lord – *"But as many as received Him, to them gave He power to become the sons of God, even to them that believe on His name: which were born, not of blood, nor of the will of the flesh, nor of the will of man, but of God" (John 1:12-13).*

When the Apostle Paul spoke of God loving and choosing to save Jacob, and God hating and passing over Esau, leaving Esau to himself, he made it clear that both Jacob and Esau deserved death and hell, but God chose to save Jacob –

Romans 9 – (13) As it is written, Jacob have I loved, but Esau have I hated. (14) What shall we say then? Is there unrighteousness with God? God forbid. (15) For He saith to Moses, I will have mercy on whom I will have mercy, and I will have compassion on whom I will have compassion. (16) So then it is not of him that willeth, nor of him that runneth, but of God that sheweth mercy.

The Bible shows how salvation is the work of all three Persons of the Godhead – Father, Son, and Holy Spirit. In the next lessons, we are going to see how –

(1) Salvation begins with God the Father, by His free and sovereign grace, choosing or electing His people in Jesus Christ unto salvation and conditioning all of their salvation upon Christ. This is the **ORIGIN** of salvation.

(2) Salvation is accomplished by Jesus Christ, the Son of God, Who became incarnate and Who, as the representative and substitute of the people given Him by the Father, obeyed the law perfectly unto the death of the cross, paid their sin-debt to God's justice, and established a perfect righteousness by which God could be just to justify them. This is the **GROUND** of salvation.

(3) Salvation is applied by God the Holy Spirit. He is sent into the world by the Father and the Son to all whom the Father chose and whom the Son redeemed. The Holy Spirit imparts spiritual life in the new birth to bring them to faith in Jesus Christ, true repentance, and the obedience of grace. He then indwells them permanently as the Spirit of life and glory. This is the **FRUIT** of salvation.

We can see that salvation as revealed in the Bible is an all-comprehensive term describing the magnitude and scope of the great salvation God freely and fully provides for His people in the Lord Jesus Christ. Most people who claim to be saved have never considered the breadth of this subject and have, consequently, missed out on the glorious truth of salvation altogether. In the following lessons, we are going to examine from the Bible what I will refer to as – THE FOUR REALMS OF SALVATION. It is very appropriate to describe all aspects of biblical salvation as REALMS because true salvation involves a kingdom of which Jesus Christ is King, and in which all who are saved are His subjects. All who are truly saved are subjects of the King and citizens of a heavenly, spiritual kingdom. These four realms are –

I. THE ETERNAL REALM OF SALVATION
II. THE LEGAL REALM OF SALVATION
III. THE SPIRITUAL REALM OF SALVATION
IV. THE GLORIFIED REALM OF SALVATION

There are three things true of all four realms of salvation:

(1) **All four realms are of the Lord** – Salvation as it is worked out, established, and applied in all four realms is all the work of God and all conditioned on the Lord Jesus Christ. No realm, aspect, or part of salvation is conditioned on sinful man. Salvation is all of God's grace in Christ and all fulfilled in and by the Lord Jesus Christ.

(2) **All four realms are necessary for the salvation of God's people** – One realm does not cancel out, deny, or diminish the reality, necessity, or glory of the others. God has freely and fully provided all aspects of salvation to accomplish His purpose in Jesus Christ for His glory.

(3) **All four realms are founded upon and centered around the Lord Jesus Christ as the salvation of His people** – Every realm of salvation exalts Christ and gives Him the preeminence He has earned as the effectual and successful Savior of His people, as the righteousness of His people to the praise of the glory of God's grace.

2

THE ETERNAL REALM
OF SALVATION

When speaking of the eternal realm of salvation, we must realize we are delving into the eternal mind and purpose of Almighty God. We must be aware that we can only go so far in this mysterious subject, because we are limited in our minds and cannot fully comprehend the infinite nature and mind of Almighty God. The Lord God Himself tell us –

Isaiah 55 – (8) For My thoughts are not your thoughts, neither are your ways My ways, saith the LORD. (9) For as the heavens are higher than the earth, so are My ways higher than your ways, and My thoughts than your thoughts.

We can only know what God reveals to us of Himself and His mind. We will not be able to understand it all or make all of it fit into our human way of reconciling truth, but we must submit to God's revelation of all things. The flaw in most people's understanding of biblical salvation is that people normally reject or deny what they cannot understand. The issue here is not what we are able to comprehend, but what does the Bible, God's inerrant, verbally inspired, holy Word, say? For example, the Bible makes it clear that before the world began, before Adam fell by disobeying God, and before he brought the whole human race into sin and death, provision had already been made for the salvation of God's people, who are called in the Bible *"God's elect" (Romans 8:33; Titus 1:1)*. This provision for the salvation of God's elect was an act of God's love, mercy, and grace towards them, and it would also be consistent with the divine claims of holiness and justice. All the details and results of the plan of mercy had been arranged and settled from the beginning by divine wisdom.

The provision of grace which God made for His people before the foundation of the world was founded upon the appointment of God's own Son to become the mediator, substitute, and surety of the covenant of salvation, also called the covenant of redemption, or the everlasting covenant of grace. This everlasting covenant was the determination and agreement that existed between the Persons of the triune Godhead – Father, Son, and Holy Spirit. It was all settled in the eternal mind of God and based on the great work of redemption the Lord Jesus Christ would come in time and accomplish for His people. This great work of redemption required the incarnation of Jesus Christ (i.e., the Son of God taking into union with His deity a perfect, sinless human nature, body and soul). This great work also required the offering of Himself as a sacrifice for sin. As the reward of His accomplishment of this great work, He would be exalted in Himself as Godman to the right hand of God. He would reign supreme over His church and over all things for His church. As supreme ruler of His church He would dispense all blessings and benefits of salvation to each one for whom He lived, died, and arose. He alone makes all of salvation effectual for God's elect given to Him before the world began.

These were all matters of definite and certain arrangement, agreed upon between the Father and His Son in the terms of the everlasting covenant. The Apostle Paul wrote of this when He described in *Ephesians 3:11* how that God designed and works all things in salvation *"according to the ETERNAL purpose which He purposed in Christ Jesus our Lord."* The same apostle also wrote of God –

2 Timothy 1 – (9) Who hath saved us, and called us with an holy calling, not according to our works, but according to His own purpose and grace, which was given us in Christ Jesus BEFORE THE WORLD

BEGAN, (10) but is now made manifest by the appearing of our Saviour Jesus Christ, Who hath abolished death, and hath brought life and immortality to light through the gospel.

Paul also wrote to his fellow minister Titus –

Titus 1 – (2) In hope of eternal life, which God, that cannot lie, promised BEFORE THE WORLD BEGAN; (3) But hath in due times manifested His word through preaching, which is committed unto me according to the commandment of God our Saviour.

The Apostle Peter wrote –

1 Peter 1 – (18) Forasmuch as ye know that ye were not redeemed with corruptible things, as silver and gold, from your vain conversation received by tradition from your fathers; (19) But with the precious blood of Christ, as of a lamb without blemish and without spot: (20) Who verily was foreordained BEFORE THE FOUNDATION OF THE WORLD, but was manifest in these last times for you, (21) Who by Him do believe in God, that raised Him up from the dead, and gave Him glory; that your faith and hope might be in God.

The eternal realm of salvation involves the origin and cause of salvation – salvation purposed and planned. Consider the following passage of Scripture in the Book of Romans –

Romans 8 – (28) And we know that all things work together for good to them that love God, to them who are the called according to His purpose. (29) For whom He did foreknow, He also did predestinate to be conformed to the image of His Son, that He might be the firstborn among many brethren. (30) Moreover whom He did predestinate, them He also called: and whom He called, them He also justified: and whom He justified, them He also glorified.

Salvation in the Bible is shown to be God's eternal purpose from the beginning. It is also shown to be the work of all three Persons of the Holy Trinity – Father, Son, and Holy Spirit. So when dealing with salvation as revealed in the Bible, we are dealing with matters both of time and eternity. We know about time as we have seen things unfold in history and in the present, but we only know what God tells us of eternity, and it is, in essence, mind-boggling. We cannot, however, deny the truth of eternity simply because our minds are limited in understanding. We must receive and submit to what God reveals to us in His Word. The Apostle Paul stated this when, by inspiration of the Holy Spirit, he wrote –

Romans 11 – (33) O the depth of the riches both of the wisdom and knowledge of God! How unsearchable are His judgments, and His ways past finding out! (34) For who hath known the mind of the Lord? Or who hath been His counsellor? (35) Or who hath first given to Him, and it shall be recompensed unto Him again? (36) For of Him, and through Him, and to Him, are all things: to Whom be glory for ever. Amen.

Some people object to this because they conclude that we do not need to study and consider these things that are so high above us. Consider, however, not only why we need to study them, but also how we who claim to be saved and to love God's Word must study them. We must study the eternal realm of salvation, FIRST, BECAUSE IT IS IN THE BIBLE –

2 Timothy 3 – (16) All scripture is given by inspiration of God, and is profitable for doctrine, for reproof, for correction, for instruction in righteousness: (17) That the man of God may be perfect, thoroughly furnished unto all good works.

We must avoid the error of natural, sinful human reasoning that causes men to ignore or even deny Scriptural truth simply because they cannot make it all reconcile with their human logic and understanding. The eternality of salvation is part of God's revealed Word, and we have no authority or right to avoid it or withhold it from others. When God reveals something to us of Himself, rest assured it is needed for our understanding of salvation and our understanding of the glory, majesty, wisdom, and power of Almighty God as He reveals Himself in our salvation. Let me give you a great example of this. God said,

"For I am the LORD, I change not; therefore ye sons of Jacob are not consumed" (Malachi 3:6). Now none of us can really understand or grasp the truth of God's immutability, that God never changes. Those who believe God changes in His nature, thoughts, or purposes think God is one like themselves, and this is idolatry. We cannot deny God's immutability because it astonishes, overwhelms, and goes far beyond our understanding. Yet, here we are told the fact that God cannot and will not change is one of the main pillars of the salvation of His people.

We need to study the eternal realm of salvation, SECONDLY, BECAUSE IT TELLS US SOMETHING OF THE CHARACTER AND NATURE OF GOD HIMSELF. This is so critical in salvation because the one who truly seeks salvation must know he is really seeking the Lord (calling upon HIS name). The one who is truly saved comes to know the true and living God as He is revealed in the Bible and not merely as we imagine Him to be. We do not want to be fooled by idols or counterfeit messiahs. The Lord Jesus Christ stated in His high priestly prayer, *"And this is life eternal, that they might know Thee the only true God, and Jesus Christ, whom Thou hast sent" (John 17:3).* We only know God as God makes Himself known. So whatever God says of Himself in His Word is truth, and truth we need to know.

We need to study the eternal realm of salvation, THIRDLY, BECAUSE IT SEALS IN OUR MINDS THE REALITY OF SALVATION BY THE POWER AND GRACE OF GOD IN THE LORD JESUS CHRIST. Jesus Christ has always been and always will be the Surety of His people as their sins were always imputed to Him and His righteousness imputed to them. This seals, in the minds of God's people, the fact that salvation is not by their works in any way, to any degree, at any stage, but only by the work of the Lord Jesus Christ, the eternal Son of God. His redemptive work on the cross has always been preeminent in the eternal mind of God. When we consider the eternal realm of salvation, we see from God's Word that the whole of salvation in time and eternity is fixed and grounded upon the glorious person and finished work of the Lord Jesus Christ. This is clearly stated in *Ephesians 1* where we read –

Ephesians 1 – (3) Blessed be the God and Father of our Lord Jesus Christ, Who hath blessed us with all spiritual blessings in heavenly places IN CHRIST: (4) According as He hath chosen us IN HIM before the foundation of the world, that we should be holy and without blame before Him in love: (5) Having predestinated us unto the adoption of children BY JESUS CHRIST to Himself, according to the good pleasure of His will, (6) To the praise of the glory of His grace, wherein He hath made us accepted IN THE BELOVED. (7) IN WHOM we have redemption THROUGH HIS BLOOD, the forgiveness of sins, according to the riches of His grace; (8) Wherein He hath abounded toward us in all wisdom and prudence; (9) Having made known unto us the mystery of His will, according to His good pleasure which He hath purposed in Himself: (10) That in the dispensation of the fullness of times He might gather together in one all things IN CHRIST, both which are in heaven, and which are on earth; even IN HIM: (11) IN WHOM also we have obtained an inheritance, being predestinated according to the purpose of Him Who worketh all things after the counsel of His own will: (12) That we should be to the praise of His glory, who first trusted IN CHRIST.

We need to study the eternal realm of salvation, FOURTHLY, BECAUSE IT REVEALS THE GLORY OF GOD IN SALVATION. All things in salvation are for the glory of God. The glory of God refers to the honor and majesty of God as He reveals Himself – Who He is, what He is like, and how He works. So in discovering the eternal God of salvation, the one true God Who saves by grace through the Lord Jesus Christ, true believers gain the assurance they are commanded as they see how God's glory demands their complete salvation. Paul called this *"THE GLORY OF GOD IN THE FACE OF JESUS CHRIST." (2 Corinthians 4:6)* He also wrote, *"For in Him dwelleth all the fullness of the Godhead bodily. And ye are complete in Him, which is the Head of all principality and power." (Colossians 2:9-10).* In the eternal realm of salvation, we are shown the absolute certainty of the complete salvation of every sinner who comes to God pleading Christ and His righteousness as the sole basis upon which he is saved. And this assurance of faith in Christ is the motivation for all Christian service and obedience. Consider the words of the Lord Jesus when He said –

John 6 – (37) All that the Father giveth Me shall come to Me; and him that cometh to Me I will in no wise cast out. (38) For I came down from heaven, not to do Mine own will, but the will of Him that sent Me. (39) And this is the Father's will which hath sent Me, that of all which He hath given Me I should lose nothing, but should raise it up again at the last day. (4) And this is the will of Him that sent Me, that every one which seeth the Son, and believeth on Him, may have everlasting life: and I will raise him up at the last day.

Consider how the Bible describes God as eternal, immutable, invincible, all-wise, and all-knowing. Consider how the Lord revealed and identified Himself to Moses as recorded in *Exodus 3* –

Exodus 3 – (13) And Moses said unto God, Behold, when I come unto the children of Israel, and shall say unto them, The God of your fathers hath sent me unto you; and they shall say to me, What is His name? what shall I say unto them? (14) And God said unto Moses, I AM THAT I AM: and He said, Thus shalt thou say unto the children of Israel, I AM hath sent me unto you.

"I AM THAT I AM" describes God as the self-existent ONE Who never changes. We must never separate salvation which is of the LORD from His nature, character, and glory. As we have already quoted from *Romans 8:28 – "And we know that all things work together for good to them that love God, to them who are the called ACCORDING TO HIS PURPOSE."* We must ask, what is God's purpose in all things? His purpose in all things is to glorify Himself, and nowhere does this shine forth more than in the salvation of His people through Jesus Christ. Again, it is all *"to the praise of the glory of His grace, wherein He hath made us accepted in the Beloved" (Ephesians 1:6).* Salvation, then, is part of the eternal mind and purpose of Almighty God. Consider more of what the Lord Jesus Himself stated of this in His high priestly prayer –

John 17 – (1) These words spake Jesus, and lifted up His eyes to heaven, and said, Father, the hour is come; glorify Thy Son, that Thy Son also may glorify Thee: (2) As Thou hast given Him power over all flesh, that He should give eternal life to as many as Thou hast given Him. (3) And this is life eternal, that they might know Thee the only true God, and Jesus Christ, whom Thou hast sent. (4) I have glorified Thee on the earth: I have finished the work which Thou gavest Me to do. (5) And now, O Father, glorify Thou Me with Thine own self with the glory which I had with Thee before the world was.

The Apostle Paul was inspired by God the Holy Spirit to write of this – *"But we speak the wisdom of God in a mystery, even the hidden wisdom, which God ordained before the world unto our glory:" (1 Corinthians 2:7)*. And as we have already read from *2 Timothy 1:9* concerning Almighty God *"Who hath saved us, and called us with an holy calling, not according to our works, but according to His own purpose and grace, which was given us in Christ Jesus before the world began."* All this is covenant language because salvation is the product of what the Bible calls the everlasting covenant of grace –

Hebrews 13 – (20) Now the God of peace, that brought again from the dead our Lord Jesus, that great shepherd of the sheep, through the blood of the everlasting covenant, (21) Make you perfect in every good work to do His will, working in you that which is wellpleasing in His sight, through Jesus Christ; to whom be glory for ever and ever. Amen.

Consider here how the blood of Jesus Christ, that blood which secures salvation for His people, is called *"the blood of the everlasting covenant."* This shows us again that the salvation of God's people was purposed and planned in the eternal, unchangeable mind of Almighty God before the world began. It shows that the salvation of sinners was always conditioned on and founded upon the redemptive work of the Lord Jesus Christ, the second Person of the Godhead. The redemptive work of Jesus Christ is described by the word *"blood"* which means His death on the cross as the surety of His people. It is the equivalent of the *"RIGHTEOUSNESS OF GOD"* revealed in the Gospel *(Romans 1:16-17; 3:21-26)*. The Gospel is the preaching of the terms of the everlasting covenant of grace, and the Lord Jesus Christ is the Surety of the everlasting covenant of grace. A surety, as it pertains to Christ in the covenant of grace, is one who guarantees payment of a debt. Jesus Christ as Surety for His people had their sin-debt imputed (charged) to Him. He became literally and legally accountable for their debt to God's justice. The payment of the debt of sin demanded His death in place of all who were given Him by God the Father in the everlasting covenant of grace. The Apostle Peter acknowledged this as he preached in Jerusalem on the day of Pentecost –

Acts 2 – (22) Ye men of Israel, hear these words; Jesus of Nazareth, a man approved of God among you by miracles and wonders and signs, which God did by Him in the midst of you, as ye yourselves also know: (23) Him, being delivered by the determinate counsel and foreknowledge of God, ye have taken, and by wicked hands have crucified and slain: (24) Whom God hath raised up, having loosed the pains of death: because it was not possible that He should be holden of it.

It is also recorded in *Acts 4 – (26) The kings of the earth stood up, and the rulers were gathered together against the Lord, and against His Christ. (27) For of a truth against Thy holy child Jesus, whom Thou hast anointed, both Herod, and Pontius Pilate, with the Gentiles, and the people of Israel, were gathered together, (28) For to do whatsoever Thy hand and Thy counsel determined before to be done.*

This was God's mind and purpose from eternity, and because Jesus Christ was and is the Surety of His people, God was able to justify them even in the Old Testament, before Christ actually came in time to redeem them. At this point you may be asking, "Is this predestination?" Many people without hesitation stop listening and reject this without thought. But do you realize that the word *"PREDESTINATE"* and other forms of it are taken directly from the Bible? Predestination in the Bible teaches us that salvation is not an afterthought with God. It is not God's plan B or contingency plan as if He were taken by surprise when Adam sinned so that God had to come up with some way to save mankind. Nothing takes God by surprise. Salvation was and is God's eternal wisdom, plan, and mind from eternity, even before the foundation of the world.

Does this mean God planned and determined the fall of man in the Garden of Eden, that He predetermined the death of His Son on the cross, and even the salvation of His people? Yes, it does, but God did it in such an infinitely wise and good way that He cannot be charged with sin or folly. God is not the author of sin, but He does overrule and dispose of all things, including sin, so as to accomplish His glory in the salvation of His people through Jesus Christ. How else could we believe that *"ALL THINGS work together for good to them that love God, to them who are the called according to His purpose." (Romans 8:28)*, or that God works *"ALL THINGS after the counsel of His own will:" (Ephesians 1:11)* Our understanding of salvation must be in tune with what God reveals, and He reveals that Christ is the one and only Surety of the salvation He purposed before the world began.

King David expressed this before His death – *"Although my house be not so with God; yet He hath made with me an everlasting covenant, ordered in all things, and sure: for this is all my salvation, and all my desire, although He make it not to grow." (2 Samuel 23:5)* The covenant of salvation would most certainly not be *"ordered in all things, and sure"* if it were conditioned on David, or any other sinner. David was expressing the blessedness of salvation by God's free and sovereign grace in and by the Lord Jesus Christ and based on Christ's righteousness imputed (charged) to David, as well as all His chosen people.

We see in all this that the eternal realm of salvation includes election unto salvation. Remember how we saw earlier in the high priestly prayer of Christ that He prayed to His Father – *"As Thou hast given Him power over all flesh, that He should give eternal life TO AS MANY AS THOU HAST GIVEN HIM." (John 17:2)* And again in *John 6* – *"All that the Father giveth Me shall come to Me; and him that cometh to Me I will in no wise cast out. For I came down from heaven, not to do Mine own will, but the will of Him that sent Me. And this is the Father's will which hath sent Me, that of all which He hath given me I should lose nothing, but should raise it up again at the last day." (John 6:37-39)* Who is He speaking of when He says, *"All that the Father giveth Me"*?

The Bible tells us He is speaking of the elect of the Lord, known as *"THE ELECTION OF GRACE" (Romans 11:5).*

The Bible teaches us that we all fell in Adam, and if left to ourselves none of us would choose God or come to Christ or call upon His name for salvation. After the Lord Jesus Christ said, *"All that the Father giveth Me shall come to Me,"* He said in *John 6:44* – *"No man can come to Me, except the Father which hath sent Me draw Him: and I will raise him up at the last day."* The word *"can"* here speaks of power or ability. Man by nature has the faculties he needs to respond positively to God's call, but he is spiritually dead and has no desire for the things of God in Christ. He is consumed with the dark powers of sin – ignorance, self-righteousness, pride, and selfishness. He has physical ears to hear the Gospel of Christ but no spiritual ears to hear it with humility, conviction, and faith. He has physical eyes to see and understand these truths with his intellect, but he has no spiritual eyes to see them with the eye of faith. The Lord spoke of this when the disciples asked Him why He spoke in parables –

Matthew 13 – (10) And the disciples came, and said unto him, Why speakest thou unto them in parables? (11) He answered and said unto them, Because it is given unto you to know the mysteries of the kingdom of heaven, but to them it is not given. (12) For whosoever hath, to him shall be given, and he shall have more abundance: but whosoever hath not, from him shall be taken away even that he hath. (13) Therefore speak I to them in parables: because they seeing see not; and hearing they hear not, neither do they understand. (14) And in them is fulfilled the prophecy of Esaias, which saith, By hearing ye shall hear, and shall not understand; and seeing ye shall see, and shall not perceive: (15) For this people's heart is waxed gross, and their ears are dull of hearing, and their eyes they have closed; lest at any time they should see with their eyes, and hear with their ears, and should understand with their heart, and should be converted, and I should heal them. (16) But blessed are your eyes, for they see: and your ears, for they hear.

No one who hears and believes the Gospel of God's grace in the Lord Jesus Christ, imagines that it was because he/she is better (less stubborn, less obstinate, less rebellious) than one who refuses to believe. Do not dare to presume to be saved because of your so-called "free will." Man's will is not free. Man's will is subject, even enslaved, to his sinful human nature and sinful desires. As men and women we are free moral agents. We make choices every day, but we choose only that which we know and desire. The Bible teaches that by nature we neither know God nor do we desire or choose the things that glorify God. This is why Christ said that sinners must be born again else they cannot see the kingdom of God *(cf. John 3:3-7)*. This is why the new birth is not by the will or works of men but by the will and power of God *(John 1:11-13)*. Man has no will to believe God, and his works are not good enough to save him.

When we study the eternal realm of salvation as revealed in the Bible, we see the Bible teaches that before the creation of the world, in eternity past, there was a covenant made between the Godhead – Father, Son, and Holy Spirit – in which God chose a people and gave them to His Son. We learn how God conditioned all of their salvation upon His Son making Him the Representative, Substitute, and Surety of His elect people. God determined to send His Son into the world to take upon Himself human nature, body and soul, without sin, and by His obedience unto death pay their sin-debt to the justice of God. In this way He would establish righteousness, the very righteousness of God, to enable God to be a just God and a Savior. Herein we are taught by God that salvation is unconditional towards sinners. All of salvation was conditioned on the Lord Jesus Christ Who came and fulfilled those conditions to the praise of the glory of God's grace. Herein we see the eternality of salvation for those whose names were written in the Lamb's Book of life before the foundation of the world *(Revelation 21:27)*.

We must also remember, however, that it is not the doctrine of election that bars sinners from salvation and entering heaven. It is man's unbelief that keeps him from salvation. The truth of election does not teach that sinners are saved even if they do not want to be saved, and it does not teach that some sinners will want to be saved but cannot because they were not elected by God. A man asked me, "Do you believe God saves sinners even when they do not want to be saved?" The answer is, NO, but we must go to the Scriptures to understand what goes on in the salvation of a sinner. The Bible teaches that no sinner by nature wants or desires salvation God's way – by free, sovereign mercy and grace in and by the Lord Jesus Christ alone. We have read this in passages such as *John 6:44* and *Romans 3:9-18*. These are just a few examples that show us the reality of man's depravity. Sinful man wants salvation, but he wants it on his own terms, like Cain of old, by works for which he can boast. When God saves a sinner, does he save that sinner even if that sinner does not want to be saved God's way? No. When God saves a sinner, God alone, by His power and grace, makes that sinner willing to believe in, rest in, and flee to the Lord Jesus Christ for all salvation – all forgiveness of sin, all righteousness, all eternal life, and all glory. He does this by the power of the Holy Spirit in the new birth as He imparts to that sinner a new knowledge, a new heart, and a new spirit *(Ezekiel 36:26-27; Hebrews 8:10-12)*. God the Holy Spirit, by the preaching of the Gospel of Christ, convinces that sinner of sin, of righteousness, and of judgment –

John 16 – (8) And when He is come, He will reprove the world of sin, and of righteousness, and of judgment: (9) Of sin, because they believe not on Me; (10) Of righteousness, because I go to my Father, and ye see Me no more; (11) Of judgment, because the prince of this world is judged.

It is under this true, invincible, Holy Spirit conviction that sinners are made more than willing to run to Christ as fast as they can and hold on for dear life. The question, then, we all need to ask and consider is this – "Do I want salvation GOD'S WAY, by His grace in the Lord Jesus Christ?" All who truly desire THIS salvation have been made willing by the power of God. The truth is anyone who desires salvation God's way, by grace through the Lord Jesus Christ, shall receive it. The Bible is clear – *"For whosoever shall call upon the name of the Lord shall be saved." (Romans 10:13)*

C H A P T E R

3

THE LEGAL REALM OF SALVATION (PART 1)

As we study the legal realm of salvation, you will find that some of what you will read, along with some of the Scripture references, have already been stated earlier in this book. This repetition is intended mainly for the purpose of emphasis and also because of the importance of having a clear understanding of this aspect of salvation. Here we will see the very heart of the Gospel message of God's grace in and by the Lord Jesus Christ. Here we will see the necessity of the Gospel truths of substitution, imputation, and satisfaction. The legal realm of salvation has to do with the ground or basis upon which God saves sinners. That ground is accomplished and established by the obedience unto death of the Lord Jesus Christ for His people, God's elect. First, recall how that in the introduction I stated that if you have never considered the question of God's justice in the forgiveness of sin, then you have never heard or believed the true Gospel of salvation by God's grace in Jesus Christ as revealed in the Bible. The moment anyone says, "God saves sinners," or "God forgives sin," there is a major theological, legal, and ethical problem that cannot be solved by man. As I also stated in the introduction, none of the major or minor religions of man have been able to solve or even come close to solving this problem. In fact, none of the major or minor religions of man even ask the question.

Think about this carefully! If God is holy, just, good, and righteous, He cannot forgive sin any more than a human judge can justly set a proven, convicted murderer free by simply saying, "I forgive you, go free." However, if I were to say that God casts all sinners into eternal damnation and death, there is no problem. God would simply be giving us as sinners what we deserve and what we have earned. This is what God's justice demands. The problem arises when we speak of salvation for sinners because God must be just in all that He does. Most people today want to avoid this issue by covering it with God's love, mercy, and grace. The fact is that salvation, as revealed in the Bible, is a marvelous act of God's love, grace, and mercy. But while He acts in love, mercy, and grace in the salvation of His people, God cannot ignore, deny, or even compromise His justice – His righteousness.

Another thing that needs to be clear in our minds is the biblical truth of righteousness. What is righteousness as revealed in God's Word? It is perfect satisfaction to God's holy law and inflexible justice. So if God forgives sinners, or if God saves sinners, He must do it in a way that honors His holiness and justice. He must do it in a righteous way. The true God of salvation is described by the following – *"He is the Rock, His work is perfect: for all His ways are judgment: a God of truth and without iniquity, just and right is He" (Deuteronomy 32:4).* God must be a just God as well as a Savior! So salvation from sin can only be attained and maintained based on perfect righteousness – perfect obedience and perfect satisfaction to God's justice. We understand, therefore, that no presumed righteousness of sinful man will do. First of all, men by nature have no righteousness before God. Secondly, because we are born spiritually dead, i.e., dead in trespasses and sin *(Ephesians 2:1-3),* and because we are sinners, we cannot produce the righteousness required by God's holy law. In fact, the Bible tells us that the best efforts of sinful man to produce righteousness always fail –

Romans 3 – (10) As it is written, There is none righteous, no, not one: (11) There is none that understandeth, there is none that seeketh after God. (12) They are all gone out of the way, they are together become unprofitable; there is none that doeth good, no, not one.

The conclusion, therefore, is –

Romans 3 – (19) Now we know that what things soever the law saith, it saith to them who are under the law: that every mouth may be stopped, and all the world may become guilty before God. (20) Therefore by the deeds of the law there shall no flesh be justified in his sight: for by the law is the knowledge of sin.

Whenever sinful men and women seek to be righteous before God by their works so as to gain or maintain salvation, they are rejected. Why? Is it because God is unreasonable, unfair, or too strict? NO! It is because God is within Himself, His very nature, holy and just, and the best works of the best of men cannot measure up to what God must require – perfect righteousness. Such efforts from sinners are acts of pride, self-righteousness, and unbelief. The Apostle Paul wrote in **Galatians 2:21** – *"I do not frustrate the grace of God: for if righteousness come by the law, then Christ is dead in vain."* Sinners who seek righteousness by their works dishonor God and deny the Person and finished work of the Lord Jesus Christ Who is the righteousness of God for His people – *"For Christ is the end of the law for righteousness to every one that believeth" (Romans 10:4).*

The main issue in salvation, then, becomes the great question of all questions – **How can sinful man be justified before God,** and, **how can a holy and just God save sinners and remain true to Himself?** Another way of stating it is – **How can God be just and still justify the ungodly?** It is in seeing and understanding the legal realm of salvation as revealed in God's Word that we come to see the answer to this great problem. The legal realm of salvation involves A SINNER'S JUSTIFICATION BEFORE GOD. To be saved is to be justified before God –

Romans 8 – (28) And we know that all things work together for good to them that love God, to them who are the called according to His purpose. (29) For whom He did foreknow, He also did predestinate to be conformed to the image of His Son, that He might be the firstborn among many brethren. (30) Moreover whom He did predestinate, them He also called: and whom He called, them he also JUSTIFIED: and whom He justified, them He also glorified.

What does it mean to be justified? The term *justify* is a legal term involving two things:

(1) To be cleared of all the guilt of sin (pronounced by God, the holy and righteous Judge, to be <u>not</u> guilty), and
(2) To be declared or pronounced righteous by God.

Whenever the Bible describes a person as *"just,"* that term can also be translated *"righteous."* An example of this is found in *Genesis 7:1 "And the LORD said unto Noah, Come thou and all thy house into the ark; for thee have I seen RIGHTEOUS before Me in this generation."* The same word is translated *"just"* in *Genesis 6:9 – "These are the generations of Noah: Noah was a JUST man and perfect in his generations, and Noah walked with God."* When Abraham was pleading for God to spare the city of Sodom, he asked – *"Wilt thou also destroy the RIGHTEOUS with the wicked?" (Genesis 18:23)* The *"righteous"* are those whom God had justified, those whom God had forgiven of all their sins, and who stand before God as *"just."* The *"wicked"* are those who are not justified.

In this justification where God declares His people righteous, we see one of the most glorious and comforting truths of salvation – God not only pardons His people, but He also brings them into His family by the adoption of grace. Consider how an earthly human king may issue a pardon to a criminal that allows the criminal to avoid suffering the punishment due to his crime, but that does not make the pardoned criminal part of the king's family. The king does not necessarily make that criminal his son and heir to his kingdom. But what if the king not only pardoned the criminal but also adopted him as his son, loving him as his son, giving him the full privileges of sonship, along with right and title to the inheritance of the kingdom? This is exactly what God does as He justifies His people. How can a holy and just God do this? He does it all by His grace based on the righteousness of the Lord Jesus Christ imputed (charged, accounted) to His people.

The legal realm of salvation describes how sinners saved by God's grace stand before Him as a holy and just God Who must judge according to truth, and how God receives them into His family and fellowship. So, again, God cannot and will not save sinners without honoring His law and justice. When God commanded Israel to look to Him, not to themselves, for salvation, He said, *"Look unto Me, and be ye saved, all the ends of the earth: for I am God, and there is none else" (Isaiah 45:22)*. Notice how God identified Himself here in *Isaiah 45:21 – "Tell ye, and bring them near; yea, let them take counsel together: who hath declared this from ancient time? who hath told it from that time? have not I the LORD? and there is no God else beside me; A JUST GOD AND A SAVIOUR; there is none beside Me."*

We have stated that the reason sinners cannot produce the righteousness required by God in salvation is because our best efforts to be holy and righteous fall short of the standard of righteousness. That standard is found in the perfect obedience and death of the Lord Jesus Christ. God's Word commands sinners to repent of their own righteousness and believe in the Lord Jesus Christ for all righteousness because –

Acts 17 – (31) Because He [God] *hath appointed a day, in the which He will judge the world in righteousness by that Man whom He hath ordained; whereof He hath given assurance unto all men, in that He hath raised Him from the dead.*

There is no doubt here the *"Man"* ordained of God is the Lord Jesus Christ. This sets forth an amazing reality concerning judgment and salvation – TO BE SAVED WE MUST BE AS RIGHTEOUS AS CHRIST HIMSELF. None of us measure up to this standard, and this is why all our best efforts to keep the law of God are iniquity. We have considered the following verses earlier, but we need to have them firmly entrenched in our minds as they describe all of us by nature and show us our need of a righteousness we cannot produce –

Romans 3 – (10) As it is written, There is none righteous, no, not one: (11) There is none that understandeth, there is none that seeketh after God. (12) They are all gone out of the way, they are together become unprofitable; there is none that doeth good, no, not one.

Romans 3 – (19) Now we know that what things soever the law saith, it saith to them who are under the law: that every mouth may be stopped, and all the world may become guilty before God. (20) Therefore by the deeds of the law there shall no flesh be justified in His sight: for by the law is the knowledge of sin.

Romans 3 – (23) For all have sinned, and come short of the glory of God;

The fact remains – OUR JUSTIFICATION BEFORE GOD IS NOT AND CANNOT BE BY OUR WORKS. This was established and revealed in the Bible right after Adam fell and brought the whole human race into sin and death. We read in *Genesis 3:7* that after Adam fell, *"And the eyes of them both were opened, and they knew that they were naked; and they sewed fig leaves together, and made themselves aprons."* Nakedness in the Bible is a metaphor for unrighteousness – shame and fear because of exposure to the wrath of God. The *"fig leaves"* were emblems of fallen man's attempts to cover himself with his own works-righteousness (self-righteousness) to hide his sin and shield himself from the wrath of God. Since the fall of man in Adam, natural man has always tried to conceal his sin either by ignoring it, justifying it, or by seeking to establish his own righteousness by his works. We see an example of this when the Lord Himself said –

Matthew 7 – (21) Not every one that saith unto Me, Lord, Lord, shall enter into the kingdom of heaven; but he that doeth the will of My Father which is in heaven. (22) Many will say to Me in that day, Lord, Lord, have we not prophesied in Thy name? and in Thy name have cast out devils? and in Thy name done many wonderful works? (23) And then will I profess unto them, I never knew you: depart from Me, ye that work iniquity.

These false professors believed that what God had enabled them to do made them righteous enough to pass the judgment of Christ. But the best works of the best of men cannot make a sinner righteous before God. And this is one of the most basic issues in salvation – **WHAT MAKES A SINNER RIGHTEOUS BEFORE GOD?** The fig leaves of our own works, even our best works, even what God enables us to do, will not make us righteous. So back in *Genesis 3*, God first gave a magnificent and gracious prophecy. It was given as God pronounced His curse upon Satan who was instrumental in bringing about the fall of man into sin, death, and condemnation.

Genesis 3 – (15) And I will put enmity between thee and the woman, and between thy seed and her seed; it shall bruise thy head, and thou shalt bruise His heel.

Who is this seed of woman? It is none other than the messiah – the Lord Jesus Christ, the anointed One Who would be the Redeemer and Savior of His people. He is the son of God, the second Person of the Holy Trinity, truly God in every attribute of His being. He is *"Emmanuel"* – *"God with us" (Matthew 1:23)*. This is the Person (one who is both God and man without sin) it would take to save God's people from their sins. It is then recorded in *Genesis 3:21* – *"Unto Adam also and to his wife did the LORD God make coats of skins, and clothed them."* Here God revealed that the only way to make reconciliation for sin is by the death of a suitable substitute in place of the sinner. Here God revealed the fact that without the shedding of blood, there is no remission of sins *(Hebrews 9:22)*. Here God established that sinners can only call upon Him, be accepted by Him, and commune with Him based on the blood of sacrifice. God established in type and picture that the only way for sinners to be saved, to be redeemed, to be justified (made righteous before God), is by the death of Jesus Christ, the Son of God in the flesh, for the sins of His people. From this point forward all the blood of lambs slain, from Abel's offering and throughout the Old Covenant times, were types, pictures, and prophecies of the Lord Jesus Christ, the Lamb of God!

Justification before God, then, has nothing to do with our works or our deeds. Justification before God is solely and totally the work of the Lord Jesus Christ in the place of all whom the Father gave Him before the foundation of the world.

4

THE LEGAL REALM
OF SALVATION
(PART 2)

One cannot properly study and clearly understand the legal realm of salvation, or any other part of salvation in the Bible, without knowing and understanding what the Bible means by *"the righteousness of God"* as revealed in the Gospel. Since the righteousness of men always falls short and will not measure up to the perfection required by God's law, what sinners need to be justified before God is summarized in this phrase – *"the righteousness of God."* The Apostle Paul wrote of this in describing the good news of salvation for sinners –

Romans 1 – (16) For I am not ashamed of the gospel of Christ: for it is the power of God unto salvation to every one that believeth; to the Jew first, and also to the Greek. (17) For therein is THE RIGHTEOUSNESS OF GOD revealed from faith to faith: as it is written, The just shall live by faith.

What exactly is this *"righteousness of God"*? It is the entire merit of the work of the Lord Jesus Christ, as the Substitute and Surety of God's elect, worked out by Him when He died on the cross paying the full penalty of all the sins of God's elect which had been imputed (charged, accounted) to Him. It is the *"righteousness OF GOD"* as it is freely and fully provided by God Himself and established by Christ Who is God and man in one Person. It is righteousness imputed without our works *(cf. Romans 4:6-8)*. It is defined by the following –

Romans 3 – (21) But now the righteousness of God without the law is manifested, being witnessed by the law and the prophets; (22) Even the righteousness of God which is by faith of Jesus Christ unto all and upon all them that believe: for there is no difference: (23) For all have sinned, and come short of the glory of God; (24) Being justified freely by His grace through the redemption that is in Christ Jesus: (25) Whom God hath set forth to be a propitiation through faith in His blood, to declare His righteousness for the remission of sins that are past, through the forbearance of God; (26) To declare, I say, at this time His righteousness: that He might be just, and the justifier of him which believeth in Jesus.

"Propitiation" is satisfaction to God's justice resulting in a total removal of God's wrath. This proves that the death of Jesus Christ was not an attempt to save all without exception but a particular redemption whereby all for whom He died are certain to be saved. Satisfaction to God's law and justice has been made for them, and their salvation is guaranteed and secured in the death of Christ which is *"the righteousness of God."* We see a contrast between man's natural inclination to seek to be justified by his own works versus God's way of justification by grace through the Lord Jesus Christ in the parable of the Pharisee and the publican –

Luke 18 – (9) And He spake this parable unto certain which trusted in themselves that they were righteous, and despised others: (10) Two men went up into the temple to pray; the one a Pharisee, and the other a publican. (11) The Pharisee stood and prayed thus with himself, God, I thank thee, that I am not as other men are, extortioners, unjust, adulterers, or even as this publican. (12) I fast twice in the week, I give tithes of all that I possess. (13) And the publican, standing afar off, would not lift up so much as his eyes unto heaven, but smote upon his breast, saying, God be merciful to me a sinner. (14) I tell you, this man went down to his house justified rather than the other: for every one that exalteth himself shall be abased; and he that humbleth himself shall be exalted.

The term *"be merciful"* can also be translated *"be propitious"* derived from the word *propitiation*. It is a word closely related to the Old Testament term *mercy seat* referring to the lid placed over the Ark of the Covenant in the Holy of Holies in the tabernacle. This is where the high priest of Israel entered on the "Day of Atonement" with the blood of sacrifice taken from the brazen altar. It signified salvation, reconciliation, and fellowship with God restored on the basis of the redemption price paid in full, or satisfaction completely made. *Propitiation* means reconciliation with God based on redemption by the blood of Jesus Christ. This is what Paul wrote of in **Romans 3**, and it is what this poor sinful publican was begging for when he cried, **"God be merciful to me a sinner."**

All of salvation, including justification before God, is on the basis of Christ (God with us) having paid the full price of redemption for all the sins of all His people. Christ met all legal obligations to the law and justice of God for all whom the Father had given Him. This is where we come to the great Gospel truths of SUBSTITUTION and IMPUTATION. Let's consider substitution first.

SUBSTITUTION

The Lord Jesus Christ is the Substitute and Surety of His people, God's elect. He stood in their place and took the punishment they deserved and earned due to sin. We have seen how God established and revealed the necessity of Christ as the one and only Substitute for sinners when He gave the first promise of the Messiah in **Genesis 3:15** and then revealed and instituted the sacrifice of animals as a picture of the death of Jesus Christ in **Genesis 3:21**. This was and is the only way of salvation for sinners, the only way God could be just and justify the ungodly. Consider Isaiah's prophecy of the Messiah –

Isaiah 53 – (5) But He was wounded for our transgressions, He was bruised for our iniquities: the chastisement of our peace was upon Him; and with His stripes we are healed. (6) All we like sheep have gone astray; we have turned every one to his own way; and the LORD hath laid on Him the iniquity of us all.

Consider how the Lord Jesus Himself spoke of it – ***John 10 – (11) I am the good shepherd: the good shepherd giveth His life for the sheep.***

The truth of the substitutionary sacrifice of Jesus Christ in the place of His people (God's elect, His sheep, His church) is at the heart of the Gospel of salvation by God's grace in Christ. Jesus Christ was not a martyr or simply a perfect example. He was the Substitute Who died under the justice and wrath of God for His people. Consider the questions – How God could justly punish His holy, innocent, and righteous Son for the sins of others; and how could He save, justify, and bless sinners based on the righteousness of another? Doesn't God's Word say, ***"He that justifieth the wicked, and he that condemneth the just, even they both are abomination to the LORD." (Proverbs 17:15).*** Yes, and here is where we see the importance of knowing and understanding the biblical truth of ...

IMPUTATION

God justified His elect, who are wicked and ungodly by nature and by practice, through the perfect righteousness of Christ imputed to them. God also condemned and punished the Lord Jesus Christ, the just ONE, through the sins of His elect imputed to Him. This was in no way a perversion of God's justice. Men make it so because they hate the doctrine of imputation, especially imputed righteousness. Why? It is because it leaves them with no room to boast in (or think highly of) themselves. The glorious truth that God justly punished His Son for sins imputed to Him and that God is just to justify sinners based on Christ's righteousness imputed to them is the heart of the Gospel, the reality of real substitution, and the glory of God's people. It is one of the major truths separating true Christianity from all false religions.

To *impute* means to "lay to the charge or account of" in the matter of the demerit or debt of sin or the merit or credit of righteousness. It has to do with one being legally and justly charged with the responsibility and liability of a debt owed or a debt paid. For example, if you were a million dollars in debt to a local bank, and you were totally bankrupt, without one penny to pay towards diminishing that debt, there would still remain one million dollars imputed or charged to your account. If you were to go to the bank and cast yourself upon their mercy, you know it would do you no good. You are in debt. The law says you are legally responsible to pay that debt. Such debt would be bondage, like being in debtor's prison. But imagine going to the bank president to beg for mercy. The bank president says, "Let's look at your account in the books." He opens the books, finds your name, and he says, to your surprise, "There is no charge here to you. You do not owe one million dollars. Someone came in and told us to put your debt on his account. He said, 'Charge it to me. I'll pay it.' And he did. It is paid – the whole amount. You owe nothing!" Could you imagine how relieved you would be? How legally free and liberated in spirit and mind you would be? But then the banker says, "Hold on, I have more information for you. That same person who paid your debt has placed one million dollars into your account. He said, 'Charge or credit it to him. This is his money which I earned and have given to him.'" You must admit that if this were to happen, you would not be able to describe your joy and peace in not only having your debt paid but also in having a million dollars imputed or credited to your account. It is the same with the doctrine of imputation when it comes to the justification of a sinner. Consider what Paul wrote of this matter –

2 Corinthians 5 – (19) To wit, that God was in Christ, reconciling the world unto Himself, NOT IMPUTING THEIR TRESPASSES UNTO THEM; and hath committed unto us the word of reconciliation. (20) Now then we are ambassadors for Christ, as though God did beseech you by us: we pray you in Christ's stead, be ye reconciled to God. (21)

For He hath made Him to be sin for us, Who knew no sin; that we might be made the righteousness of God in Him.

God does not impute trespasses to His people. He does not charge them with sin or its debt. To whom did God charge them? He charged them to Jesus Christ as the Substitute and Surety of His people. God the Father *"made Him to be sin for us."* This is the imputation of the debt of the sins of God's elect to Christ. Again, some say that it would be unjust for God to do this because Christ did no sin and knew no sin, but they fail to see the reality of real substitution and what it is to be a surety. A surety is one who willingly takes responsibility for another's debt. In the everlasting covenant of grace, the Lord Jesus Christ willingly agreed to take responsibility for the sins, the debt, of His people. We see an illustration of this in the book of *Philemon*. A slave named Onesimus had robbed and fled from his master, Philemon. But in the providence of God Onesimus was led to the Apostle Paul who preached the Gospel of Christ to him, and he was converted to Christ. So Paul interceded with Philemon on behalf of Onesimus –

Philemon – (18) If he hath wronged thee, or oweth thee ought, put that on mine account; (19) I Paul have written it with mine own hand, I will repay it: albeit I do not say to thee how thou owest unto me even thine own self besides.

Should Philemon have written back to Paul and said, "Paul, I can't do that because it would be illegal, unjust, or dishonest." NO! Well, in the same way, the Lord Jesus Christ willingly stood as Surety for His people and willingly took the whole responsibility for all their sins.

This great truth of imputation goes even further to show that as the sins of God's elect were imputed to Christ, they (God's elect) are *"made the RIGHTEOUSNESS OF GOD in Him."* This speaks of the imputation of righteousness to all God's elect in and by the Lord Jesus Christ. It is God legally and justly declaring the reality of righteousness to His people in Christ. To be in Christ is to be in Him:

(1) BY GOD'S ELECTING GRACE WHEN HE CHOSE HIS PEOPLE IN CHRIST BEFORE THE FOUNDATION OF THE WORLD.

(2) BY GOD'S REDEEMING GRACE WHEN CHRIST DIED FOR THEIR SINS AND ESTABLISHED RIGHTEOUSNESS FOR THEM.

(3) BY GOD'S REGENERATING GRACE WHEN THEY ARE BORN AGAIN BY THE SPIRIT AND BROUGHT TO FAITH IN CHRIST.

All who are IN CHRIST are completely cleared of the guilt of sin. Their debt to God's justice has been paid in full by the Lord Jesus Christ in His obedience unto death for them. It means that they cannot be condemned for sin, and that they cannot be charged with sin so as to be condemned –

Romans 8 – (33) Who shall lay any thing to the charge of God's elect? it is God that justifieth. (34) Who is he that condemneth? It is Christ that died, yea rather, that is risen again, who is even at the right hand of God, who also maketh intercession for us.

All who believe in the Lord Jesus Christ have been *"made the righteousness of God in Him."* They have been reconciled to God on the ground of Christ's righteousness imputed to them. This was expressed by the prophet Jeremiah –

Jeremiah 23 – (5) Behold, the days come, saith the LORD, that I will raise unto David a righteous Branch, and a King shall reign and prosper, and shall execute judgment and justice in the earth. (6) In his days Judah shall be saved, and Israel shall dwell safely: and this is his name whereby HE shall be called, THE LORD OUR RIGHTEOUSNESS.

The reality of being justified before God is that we who are in Christ are truly cleared of all guilt, forgiven of all sin, and we truly stand righteous before God, in His sight, even though we are still sinners within ourselves. Paul expressed this so clearly in the *Book of Romans.*

In *Romans 6:1-9* he makes the point that we who are saved are *"dead to sin,"* meaning justified in Christ. We are dead to sin's power to condemn us. But Paul went on to write –

Romans 6 – (12) Let not sin therefore reign in your mortal body, that ye should obey it in the lusts thereof. (13) Neither yield ye your members as instruments of unrighteousness unto sin: but yield yourselves unto God, as those that are alive from the dead, and your members as instruments of righteousness unto God.

The reality of being justified before God is the non-imputation of sin to His people and the imputation of Christ's righteousness to them, so that they can say with the Apostle Paul –

Romans 7 – (24) O wretched man that I am! who shall deliver me from the body of this death? (25) I thank God through Jesus Christ our Lord. So then with the mind I myself serve the law of God; but with the flesh the law of sin.
Romans 8 – (1) There is therefore now no condemnation to them which are in Christ Jesus, who walk not after the flesh, but after the Spirit.

This is why Paul expressed his desire even in old age –

Philippians 3 – (8) Yea doubtless, and I count all things but loss for the excellency of the knowledge of Christ Jesus my Lord: for whom I have suffered the loss of all things, and do count them but dung, that I may win Christ, (9) And be found in Him, not having mine own righteousness, which is of the law, but that which is through the faith of Christ, the righteousness which is of God by faith: (10) That I may know Him, and the power of His resurrection, and the fellowship of his sufferings, being made conformable unto His death; (11) If by any means I might attain unto the resurrection of the dead.

As I stated before, there are many who attack this great truth of imputation by claiming it is a "legal fiction." They portray it as God declaring one righteous when that person is really not righteous. But this is a serious misunderstanding of the legal realm of salvation and the reality of justification before God based on Jesus Christ's righteousness imputed to His people. Remember, God the Father punished His holy, harmless, undefiled, sinless Son, based on sin imputed to Him. That was no legal fiction –

Galatians 3 – (13) Christ hath redeemed us from the curse of the law, BEING MADE A CURSE FOR US: for it is written, Cursed is every one that hangeth on a tree:

1 Peter 3 – (18) For Christ also hath once suffered for sins, the just for the unjust, that he might bring us to God, being put to death in the flesh, but quickened by the Spirit:

Also, remember, that where God imputes righteousness to His people in and by the Lord Jesus Christ, He also sends the Holy Spirit to impart spiritual life in the new birth evidenced by faith in Christ and true repentance. The justification of a sinner before God is purely a legal matter, but salvation is more than justification alone. The sinner's justification before God legally by the righteousness of God in Christ imputed always issues forth in the new birth, spiritual life given, imparted, by the Holy Spirit to each and every one of God's elect in each successive generation. However, we must keep this distinction:

(1) THE WORK OF CHRIST ON THE CROSS FOR HIS PEOPLE IS THE ONLY GROUND OF SALVATION.

(2) THE WORK OF CHRIST IN THE NEW BIRTH WITHIN HIS PEOPLE BY THE HOLY SPIRIT IS THE FRUIT OF SALVATION

Let's consider an exercise in Biblical interpretation to help us see this. King David was inspired by the Holy Spirit to write –

Psalm 32 – (1) Blessed is he whose transgression is forgiven, whose sin is covered. (2) Blessed is the man unto whom the LORD imputeth not iniquity, and in whose spirit there is no guile.

Here we see three words to describe sin:

(1) *"Transgression" (pesha`)* which carries the idea of rebellion against God, breaking God's law. The New Testament Greek equivalent is ἀνομία, pronounced *ä-no-mē'-ä*, which means breaking God's law – *"sin is the transgression of the law" (1 John 3:4b)*.

(2) *"Sin" (chata'ah)* which carries the implication of that which is deserving of punishment. In the New Testament, the equivalent is ἁμαρτία, pronounced *hä-mär-tē'-ä*, which means to miss the mark or fall short of the requirement – *"For He hath made Him to be sin for us" (2 Corinthians 5:21a)*.

(3) *"Iniquity" (`avon)* which carries the idea of being perverse, crooked, twisted, or imbalanced. The New Testament equivalent in Greek is ἀνομία, pronounced *ä-no-mē'-ä*, which means without or against the law of God as in that which does not balance with or equal the standard of righteousness found in the law of God – *"depart from Me, ye that work iniquity" (Matthew 7:23b)*.

Many people think of and describe sin as if it were a substance or thing, something like a solid, liquid, or gas. Some even imagine it to be a physical entity such as a germ in our bodies or in the blood stream. But sin is none of these things. Sin is breaking the law of God; sin is missing the mark; sin is not being equal to the requirement. All sin, in whatever way it is described in God's Word, deserves death and damnation.

The word *"forgiven"* means "to lift up, to bear, to carry, or to carry away." We have emphasized how the forgiveness of sin by Almighty God must be based on satisfaction to His justice. David recognized this as expressed in the phrase – *"whose sin is covered."* The word *"covered"* means "to conceal or hide from view," but not simply to cover over sin without dealing with it and its consequences. It is not merely that sin is still there but only hidden from view. How are they hidden from God's view? David explains how in *verse 2 – "Blessed is the man unto whom the LORD imputeth not iniquity."* God does not view David's sin in the sense that He does not impute or charge David with the guilt and penalty of sin. In his own confession David still owns and acknowledges his sinfulness, – *"I acknowledged my sin unto thee, and mine iniquity have I not hid. I said, I will confess my transgressions unto the LORD;*

and thou forgavest the iniquity of my sin" (Psalm 32:5) – but he trusts the LORD not to impute sin to him. This is not a pretense on God's part or some kind of legal fiction. This non-imputation of sin includes three glorious realities:

(1) The non-imputation of sin to God's people means the imputation of their sin(s) to the Lord Jesus Christ. God had to do something with the debt of sin. He could not simply forget or ignore it. He must be just when He justifies. Someone must pay the penalty. How did God do this? Read again the following –

2 Corinthians 5 – (18) And all things are of God, Who hath reconciled us to Himself by Jesus Christ, and hath given to us the ministry of reconciliation; (19) To wit, that God was in Christ, reconciling the world unto Himself, NOT IMPUTING THEIR TRESPASSES UNTO THEM; and hath committed unto us the word of reconciliation. (20) Now then we are ambassadors for Christ, as though God did beseech you by us: we pray you in Christ's stead, be ye reconciled to God. (21) For He hath made Him to be sin for us, Who knew no sin; that we might be made the righteousness of God in Him.

The Lord Jesus Christ was *"made sin"* by the imputation of the sin(s) of God's elect to Him. The guilt, curse, and debt of their sins were legally charged to Him so much so that their sins became His own *(cf. Psalm 40:12; 69:5)*, not by impartation, not by contamination, but only by imputation. Christ was never made to be a sinner or sinful, and neither was He ever made, as one man says, "the thing itself." As stated, sin is not a "thing." Christ was *"made a curse"* for His people *(Galatians 3:13)* and, therefore, bore their *"sins in His own body on the tree"* (1 Peter *2:24)*. This imputation of the guilt and penalty of sin(s) to Christ was so real that He came under the wrath of His Father, suffered, bled, and died to pay the full debt due unto God's justice for their sins. It was so real that He was forsaken of His Father in His time on the cross *(Psalm 22:1; Matthew 27:46)*.

(2) The non-imputation of sin to God's people means the imputation of righteousness to all for whom Christ lived, died, and rose. It is possible for a person to take upon himself another person's debt and pay it in full without giving that person any more money to put to their account. But that is not the way God works in the justification of His people according to the terms of the everlasting covenant of grace. With God, in the justification of His people, the non-imputation of sin automatically means the imputation of righteousness to them. As Christ was *"made sin,"* all for whom He died are *"made the righteousness of God in Him."* Consider what God the Holy Spirit inspired the Apostle Paul to write in the **Book of Romans** as a commentary upon David's words in **Psalm 32:1-2** –

Romans 4 – (6) Even as David also describeth the blessedness of the man, unto whom God imputeth righteousness without works, (7) Saying, Blessed are they whose iniquities are forgiven, and whose sins are covered. (8) Blessed is the man to whom the Lord will not impute sin.

When David wrote **Psalm 32:1-2**, he did not use the term *"righteousness,"* but we are told by God Who inspired Paul to write these words that this is what David had in mind and meant when he wrote of the non-imputation of sin. The blessed person to whom God does not impute iniquity has righteousness imputed to him without works. In other words, his sin was charged to Christ, and Christ's righteousness was charged to him with no consideration, help, or addition of his own works. It is all of God's free and sovereign grace in Christ Jesus. And though this blessed person, while living on this earth, is still a sinner in himself, he has no sin charged to him by God. This is how all who believe in the Lord Jesus Christ can say, **"Herein is our love made perfect, that we may have boldness in the day of judgment: because as He is, so are we in this world"** (1 John 4:17).

David did not see this as a "legal fiction" but as a blessing from Almighty God in the Lord Jesus Christ. As the Substitute and Surety of His people, the Lord Jesus Christ died and satisfied the justice of God against them, and He reconciled them unto God by establishing the only righteousness whereby God could be both a just God and a Savior – the righteousness of God in Christ freely imputed to them. This is the very ground of all salvation for the people of God.

(3) The non-imputation of sin and the imputation of Christ's righteousness to God's people mean the impartation of spiritual life to all of God's people in each successive generation. Where Jesus Christ has put away the sins of His people by the sacrifice of Himself, and where His righteousness has been imputed to His people by Almighty God, the Holy Spirit is sent to impart spiritual life, knowledge, and all graces and fruit of the Spirit to their persons. They must be and will be born again. David expressed this in *Psalm 32:2* when he added, *"and in whose spirit there is no guile."* *"Spirit"* here is the new heart and new spirit created within a person by the Holy Spirit in regeneration and conversion. *"Guile"* is dishonesty and deception that keeps sinners ignorant of their own depravity, of God's holiness and justice, and of the only way of salvation by the grace of God in and by the Lord Jesus Christ. This is the *"spirit"* of grace, faith, repentance, love, obedience, and gratitude whereby the Holy Spirit brings a sinner to Jesus Christ in faith –

Romans 10 – (4) For Christ is the end of the law for righteousness to every one that believeth … (10) For with the heart man believeth unto righteousness; and with the mouth confession is made unto salvation.

This involves the spiritual realm of salvation, and it is the subject of the next two chapters of our study.

CHAPTER

5

THE SPIRITUAL REALM OF SALVATION (PART 1)

The spiritual realm of salvation is the specific work of God in applying salvation to each and every one of His elect people personally in each successive generation. It is the sovereign, powerful, and invincible work of God the Holy Spirit beginning with the new birth (regeneration and conversion) as He imparts spiritual life, knowledge, grace, and fruit of the Spirit. This work of the Holy Spirit continues throughout the lives of God's elect to preserve them and bring them to be finally and fully glorified. In the spiritual realm of salvation a born-again person, indwelt by the Holy Spirit and by the power and grace of God in Jesus Christ, lives the resurrected, spiritual life of faith, repentance, and obedience as a willing, loving bond-servant of Christ. The work of the Holy Spirit in the spiritual realm of salvation is the fruit, effect, and result of the work of Jesus Christ in the legal realm of salvation where He established the ground of justification and eternal life for His people. The Apostle Paul described this in the following verses of Scripture –

Galatians 2 – (19a) For I through the law am dead to the law,

To be *"dead to the law"* means to be justified before God, cleared of all guilt and declared righteous in and by the Lord Jesus Christ. Justification before God based on the righteousness of Christ imputed (charged) is the ground of salvation, but it is not the whole of salvation. Salvation does not end with justification. It continues with living a spiritual life –

Galatians 2 – (19b) that I might live unto God.

This describes a born-again person living the resurrected, spiritual life of faith in and love for the Lord Jesus Christ. How did all this come about, and how does it work out in the lives of God's people?

Galatians 2 – (20) I am crucified with Christ: nevertheless I live; yet not I, but Christ liveth in me: and the life which I now live in the flesh I live by the faith of the Son of God, Who loved me, and gave Himself for me. (21) I do not frustrate the grace of God: for if righteousness come by the law, then Christ is dead in vain.

Righteousness for justification and spiritual life in the new birth both come from and by the Lord Jesus Christ, not from ourselves – neither our works nor our wills. Let's begin by putting these things in their proper perspective and studying the Scriptures which teach what we have stated before – SPIRITUAL LIFE IS THE FRUIT, THE RESULT, THE EFFECT OF THE CROSS-WORK OF CHRIST –

John 12 – (32) And I, if I be lifted up from the earth, will draw all men unto Me. (33) This He said, signifying what death He should die.

The death of Jesus Christ not only secures the righteousness that is imputed for a sinner's legal justification, but it also secures spiritual life that is imparted, beginning with the new birth where Christ draws all for whom He died to Himself in faith.

John 16 – (7) Nevertheless I tell you the truth; It is expedient for you that I go away: for if I go not away, the Comforter will not come unto you; but if I depart, I will send Him unto you. (8) And when He is come, He will reprove the world of sin, and of righteousness, and of judgment:

Consider the following: (1) The cross work of Jesus Christ for His people is the ground of salvation. The merit of His work alone, imputed to His people, is their righteousness before Holy God. (2) The work of the Holy Spirit in His people is not a work that makes them righteous before God. Again, it is only Christ's work on the cross that makes His people righteous in God's sight. But the Holy Spirit's work in God's people brings them to see and submit to Christ as their righteousness before God. (3) Before God's people are ever born again by the Holy Spirit, they are already justified before God in and by the Lord Jesus Christ. When the Holy Spirit imparts spiritual life, it can be said that God's people are justified in their conscience as they are brought to see and believe in the Lord Jesus Christ and His work to remove the guilt of sin legally –

Hebrews 10 – (19) Having therefore, brethren, boldness to enter into the holiest by the blood of Jesus, (20) By a new and living way, which He hath consecrated for us, through the veil, that is to say, His flesh; (21) And having an high priest over the house of God; (22) Let us draw near with a true heart in full assurance of faith, having our hearts sprinkled from an evil conscience, and our bodies washed with pure water.

The Apostle Paul stated this in *Romans 8 – (10) And if Christ be in you, the body is dead because of sin; but the Spirit is life because of righteousness.*

Spiritual life comes as the result of righteousness worked out by (and found only in) the obedience unto death of the Lord Jesus Christ. Jesus Christ indwells His people spiritually by the Holy Spirit and by His Word because of what He has accomplished for His people on the cross. The Bible teaches that all who are justified are *"justified freely by His grace through the redemption that is in Christ Jesus:" (Romans 3:24).* But, again, it also teaches that salvation does not end with justification. The Scriptures show us that all who are justified in and by Christ, based on His righteousness imputed, will without fail be born again by the Holy Spirit, brought to faith in Christ, and live by the grace and power of God unto final glory –

Romans 5 – (1) Therefore being justified, by faith we have peace with God through our Lord Jesus Christ:

Peace with God is founded upon the righteousness of God in Jesus Christ imputed. The knowledge and experience of that peace within the justified sinner's heart come by God-given faith in Jesus Christ Who established peace for all who believe in Him.

Romans 15 – (13) Now the God of hope fill you with all joy and peace in believing, that ye may abound in hope, through the power of the Holy Ghost.

It is a great blessing to be cleared of all charges and to be declared righteous in God's sight. It is also a great blessing of God's love and grace in the Lord Jesus Christ for sinners to be brought into and permanently made part of God's spiritual family. It is another great blessing of God's mercy and grace in Christ Jesus to be spiritually born again, literally, raised from the dead, and given a new heart, a new spirit, a new song as a true child of God. There is a sense in which all who are children of God have always been His children in the eternal realm of salvation. They were all chosen in Christ, their elder Brother, before the foundation of the world and justified by Him as their Surety through His finished work in time on the cross. But even the elect of God fell into sin and death in Adam. And because of that fall, even God's elect are born dead in trespasses and sins with a fallen, sinful human nature.

Ephesians 2 – (1) And you hath He quickened, who were dead in trespasses and sins; (2) Wherein in time past ye walked according to the course of this world, according to the prince of the power of the air, the spirit that now worketh in the children of disobedience: (3) Among whom also we all had our conversation in times past in the lusts of our flesh, fulfilling the desires of the flesh and of the mind; and were by nature the children of wrath, even as others.

By nature even the elect of God aligned themselves with Satan. In essence by nature Satan is the father of all who fell in Adam. So we come to understand that not all people are in God's spiritual, eternal family. GOD IS NOT THE SPIRITUAL FATHER OF ALL WITHOUT EXCEPTION. Remember what Christ told the Pharisees –

John 8 – (44) Ye are of your father the devil, and the lusts of your father ye will do. He was a murderer from the beginning, and abode not in the truth, because there is no truth in him. When he speaketh a lie, he speaketh of his own: for he is a liar, and the father of it. (45) And because I tell you the truth, ye believe me not.

How does a sinner become part of God's spiritual family? It is by:

(1) ELECTION IN CHRIST (God choosing them before the foundation of the world);

(2) REDEMPTION IN CHRIST (Christ paying their sin-debt in full and establishing righteousness whereby God can be just to justify them);

(3) ADOPTION IN CHRIST (which is the adoption of grace). We see this clearly in *Ephesians 1* where Paul wrote:

Ephesians 1 – (3) Blessed be the God and Father of our Lord Jesus Christ, Who hath blessed us with all spiritual blessings in heavenly places in Christ: (4) According as He hath chosen us in Him before the foundation of the world, that we should be holy and without blame before Him in love: (5) Having predestinated us unto the adoption of children by Jesus Christ to Himself, according to the good pleasure of His will, (6) To the praise of the glory of His grace, wherein He hath made us accepted in the beloved. (7) In whom we have redemption through His blood, the forgiveness of sins, according to the riches of His grace;

(4) NEW BIRTH IN AND BY CHRIST (Christ sending the Holy Spirit to apply His grace to His people). As we read in *Galatians 4* –

Galatians 4 – (4) But when the fulness of the time was come, God sent forth his Son, made of a woman, made under the law, (5)

To redeem them that were under the law, that we might receive the adoption of sons. (6) And because ye are sons, God hath sent forth the Spirit of his Son into your hearts, crying, Abba, Father. (7) Wherefore thou art no more a servant, but a son; and if a son, then an heir of God through Christ.

So in the eternal realm of salvation, God chose His people and predestined them to be conformed to the image of His Son. In the legal realm of salvation God eternally justified them in Christ, their Surety, and in time redeemed them by the blood of Christ, thus, establishing the ground of justification. In the spiritual realm of salvation God gives them spiritual life and brings them into His spiritual family and fellowship by Christ, thus, establishing them as His children and heirs.

We can see here how the spiritual realm of salvation, the necessity of spiritual life imparted, answers one of the major objections that unbelievers bring against the eternal realm of salvation. Recall how in the eternal realm we spoke of salvation as a sinner's election by God in Christ. This took place before the world began in the eternal mind and purpose of God. Some object to this by saying, "Then it does not matter what I do or don't do. If I am one of God's elect I will be saved no matter what, and if I am not one of God's elect, I will not be saved no matter what." The Bible states otherwise.

First, the Bible says, *"The secret things belong unto the LORD our God: but those things which are revealed belong unto us and to our children for ever, that we may do all the words of this law" (Deuteronomy 29:29).* Whom God has chosen before the foundation of the world and whom He has passed by is most certainly one of those *"secret things"* that belong to Him, not us.

Secondly, the Bible also reveals that all whom God chose before the foundation of the world will seek the Lord and find Him in salvation. They will do this by believing in Him through God-given faith under the preaching of the Gospel of Christ in the power of the Holy Spirit. The Holy Spirit uses means to apply this salvation, and He begins by bringing God's elect under the preaching of the Gospel in power –

1 Thessalonians 1 – (4) Knowing, brethren beloved, your election of God. (5) For our gospel came not unto you in word only, but also in power, and in the Holy Ghost, and in much assurance; as ye know what manner of men we were among you for your sake.

2 Thessalonians 2 – (13) But we are bound to give thanks alway to God for you, brethren beloved of the Lord, because God hath from the beginning chosen you to salvation through sanctification of the Spirit and belief of the truth: (14) Whereunto he called you by our gospel, to the obtaining of the glory of our Lord Jesus Christ.

Here is where we learn that election itself is not salvation, but election is unto salvation.

Thirdly, the Bible teaches that election can only be known by the calling –

2 Peter 1 – (10) – Wherefore the rather, brethren, give diligence to make your calling and election sure: for if ye do these things, ye shall never fall:

Recall again how the legal realm of salvation describes a sinner's justification before God. Justification is a legal work of redemption based on the sins of God's elect imputed (charged) to Lord Jesus Christ for which He suffered, bled, and died, in payment of their debt to God's justice. It is the imputation of His righteousness, the entire merit of His obedience unto death, to their persons whereby God is just to justify them. Justification is totally a work of Christ FOR His people and has nothing to do with our works or even our experience. Christ alone, by Himself, suffered unto death as the Representative, Substitute, and Surety of all God's elect –

Hebrews 1 – (3) Who being the brightness of His glory, and the express image of His person, and upholding all things by the word of His power, when He had BY HIMSELF purged our sins, sat down on the right hand of the Majesty on high;

Hebrews 10 – (10) By the which will we are sanctified through the offering of the body of Jesus Christ once for all. (14) For by one offering he hath perfected for ever them that are sanctified.

However, as we have been showing in this whole series of studies, when we speak of salvation as set forth in the Bible, we see that the legal realm, a sinner's justification before Holy God, is not the only realm. Salvation also includes the spiritual realm – the work of God the Holy Spirit in His people. What God has purposed before the foundation of the world in the ETERNAL REALM of salvation, and what Christ has purchased on the cross by His work of redemption as Substitute and Surety in the LEGAL REALM of salvation, has its fruit or result in the work of the Holy Spirit in the SPIRITUAL REALM of salvation.

Now bear with me as I repeat the definition of the spiritual realm of salvation. It refers to the sovereign, powerful, necessary work of God the Holy Spirit in the application of salvation, spiritual life and grace, to each of God's elect in each successive generation. The spiritual realm begins with a person's experience in the new birth as he or she is regenerated, or given spiritual life, by the Holy Spirit and converted to Christ. It is a sinner being brought to faith in Christ and repentance of dead works. So then, not only must a sinner be chosen of God and justified legally in salvation, i.e. set free from condemnation and wrath, he must be set free from spiritual death and darkness. In the spiritual realm of salvation sinners are brought by God to experience and know of that salvation within themselves – their minds, affections, and wills – their hearts. This realm of salvation is a heart work.

YOU MUST BE BORN AGAIN

Some people often refer to the new birth as salvation itself because this is when a person first comes to know and personally experience salvation by the grace of God in the Lord Jesus Christ. The spiritual realm of salvation begins with the new birth, but it does not stop there. It continues with perseverance in the faith, not by our own power and goodness, but by the power and goodness of Almighty God in and by the Lord Jesus Christ.

Let's first consider the new birth. The Bible teaches that no one becomes a true Christian until the Holy Spirit gives that person spiritual life in regeneration and brings that person to a saving knowledge of (and faith in) the Lord Jesus Christ in conversion. This is why the Bible often repeats the Gospel commandment of faith which basically states *believe on the Lord Jesus Christ, and you shall be saved.* No one will be saved without believing in the Lord Jesus Christ. But people have come to misunderstand both the cause and the nature of true faith. For example, many believe that faith is the exercise of man's free will and that all men have some spark or degree of faith so that all that is needed is some form of gentle persuasion to get them to accept Jesus as their personal Savior and give their lives to Him. But this is not the case. Paul quoted God's declaration to Moses in **Romans 9:15-16** where God declared, *"... I will have mercy on whom I will have mercy, and I will have compassion on whom I will have compassion. So then it is not of him that willeth, nor of him that runneth, but of God that showeth mercy."*

So salvation, including faith, is a free gift that comes by the sovereign will, power, mercy, and grace of God, not by the sinner's will. The natural man's will is not free but in bondage to sin and ignorance –

1 Corinthians 2 – (14) But the natural man receiveth not the things of the Spirit of God: for they are foolishness unto him: neither can he know them, because they are spiritually discerned.

Many believe man has a free will because we make choices in life every day. We decide what to eat or not to eat, what to wear, not to wear. We even make moral choices in so many areas of life. But this only proves that we are free to choose what we know and what we desire. The Bible teaches that by nature none of us know the way of salvation by God's grace in Christ and that none of us desire God's way because it will not give us any room to boast in the matter of salvation.

It is not our free will choice that makes the difference between saved and lost. IT IS GOD'S GRACE ALONE IN CHRIST! Salvation is not accomplished within us by the gentle persuasion of the preachers but by the sovereign power of God the Holy Spirit, irresistibly drawing sinners to Christ and imparting spiritual life, knowledge, grace, even faith into their hearts. It is a resurrection from the dead by the will and power of God in Christ. In the Bible this miraculous work of the Holy Spirit is called being born again or born from above. The Lord Jesus Christ spoke of it in *John 3* when He told Nicodemus –

John 3 – (3) Verily, verily, I say unto thee, Except a man be born again, he cannot see the kingdom of God. (4) Nicodemus saith unto him, How can a man be born when he is old? can he enter the second time into his mother's womb, and be born? (5) Jesus answered, Verily, verily, I say unto thee, Except a man be born of water and of the Spirit, he cannot enter into the kingdom of God. (6) That which is born of the flesh is flesh; and that which is born of the Spirit is spirit. (7) Marvel not that I said unto thee, Ye must be born again.

Consider what the Bible teaches of this new birth –

(1) The new birth is necessary because we all by nature are spiritually dead in trespasses and sins. The Bible teaches that all of us by nature, as we fell in Adam into sin and death, and as we are born naturally into this world, are spiritually dead in trespasses and sins. Now as we read the following verses of Scripture, let's ask ourselves, "Who is he describing here?"

Ephesians 2 – (1) And you hath He quickened, who were dead in trespasses and sins; (2) Wherein in time past ye walked according to the course of this world, according to the prince of the power of the air, the spirit that now worketh in the children of disobedience: (3) Among whom also we all had our conversation in times past in the lusts of our flesh, fulfilling the desires of the flesh and of the mind; and were by nature the children of wrath, even as others.

This passage teaches us that by nature there is no difference between those whom God chose and those whom God passed by. No sinner deserves or can earn salvation.

Romans 3 – (9) What then? are we better than they? No, in no wise: for we have before proved both Jews and Gentiles, that they are all under sin; (10) As it is written, There is none righteous, no, not one: (11) There is none that understandeth, there is none that seeketh after God. (12) They are all gone out of the way, they are together become unprofitable; there is none that doeth good, no, not one.

When we speak of spiritual death, we are speaking of what is known as the total depravity and inability of man. Total depravity does not teach that all men and women are as bad as we could be. Could you imagine what kind of world this would be if we were all let go to fulfill our sinful desires and goals? Total depravity teaches that all of us fell in Adam and sin has affected us in every part of our being – our minds, affections, and our wills (our very hearts) so that if left to ourselves, we will not seek the Lord.

John 6 – (44) No man can come to Me, except the Father which hath sent Me draw him: and I will raise him up at the last day.

The inability here is not a physical or even a moral inability as to the faculties of the soul. In other words, we all by nature have minds, affections, and wills, even consciences *(cf. Romans 2:14-15)*, but we are unable to seek the Lord and believe in the Lord Jesus Christ for salvation because we are spiritually dead, meaning we have no knowledge of God's way of salvation by grace in Christ, and we have no desire to believe and submit to God's way of salvation. Our hearts are full of human pride, self-love, and self-will. Like Cain of old, we have a natural religious desire to approach God, appease Him, and be accepted of Him, but we want all of this OUR way, not GOD'S WAY in Christ. This is why the evil spirit of human works and free-will religion under the guise of "Christianity" pervades and dominates our day.

The reason we must be born again by the Holy Spirit is that we must be given what we by nature do not have – spiritual life, knowledge, desires, all evidencing what the Bible calls *"a new heart"* and *"a new spirit" (Ezekiel 26:26)*, a circumcised heart *(Deuteronomy 30:6;*

Romans 2:28-29), and *"the washing of regeneration" (Titus 3:5)*. This is the new birth in the spiritual realm of salvation.

(2) The new birth is a sovereign powerful work of God the Holy Spirit by the will and word of God –

John 1 – (11) He came unto His own, and His own received Him not. (12) But as many as received Him, to them gave He power to become the sons of God, even to them that believe on His name: (13) Which were born, not of blood, nor of the will of the flesh, nor of the will of man, but of God.

The new birth is the invincible, irresistible calling of the Holy Spirit through the preaching of the Gospel of Christ. It only occurs under the preaching of the true Gospel of Christ, not a false gospel –

Romans 1 – (16) For I am not ashamed of the gospel of Christ: for it is the power of God unto salvation to every one that believeth; to the Jew first, and also to the Greek. (17) For therein is the righteousness of God revealed from faith to faith: as it is written, The just shall live by faith.

Romans 10 – (13) For whosoever shall call upon the name of the Lord shall be saved. (14) How then shall they call on Him in Whom they have not believed? and how shall they believe in Him of Whom they have not heard? and how shall they hear without a preacher? (15) And how shall they preach, except they be sent? as it is written, How beautiful are the feet of them that preach the gospel of peace, and bring glad tidings of good things! (16) But they have not all obeyed the gospel. For Esaias saith, Lord, who hath believed our report? (17) So then faith cometh by hearing, and hearing by the word of God.

The Lord Jesus told His disciples, *"But blessed are your eyes, for they see: and your ears, for they hear" (Matthew 13:16)*. Do you suppose that these disciples saw and heard the truth because they were better people than those who refused to see and hear it? NO! Their spiritual sight and hearing was totally by God's grace – *"Because it is given unto you to know the mysteries of the kingdom of heaven, but to them it is not given" (Matthew 13:11).*

The people of God are identified as THE CALLED – *"And we know that all things work together for good to them that love God, to them who are THE CALLED according to His purpose" (Romans 8:28).* The reason this calling is so powerful and irresistible is because it is by the power of the Holy Spirit in true conviction –

John 16 – (8) And when He is come, He will reprove the world of sin, and of righteousness, and of judgment: (9) Of sin, because they believe not on Me; (10) Of righteousness, because I go to my Father, and ye see Me no more; (11) Of judgment, because the prince of this world is judged.

(3) The new birth is liberation from spiritual death and darkness. Consider the words of the Apostle Paul in *Romans 6* –

Romans 6 – (17) But God be thanked, that ye were the servants of sin, but ye have obeyed from the heart that form of doctrine which was delivered you. (18) Being then made free from sin, ye became the servants of righteousness.

This speaks of freedom in the sense of liberation from spiritual death and darkness whereby sinners are enabled to believe in Christ for all their salvation and serve Him as motivated by grace, love, and gratitude. They are not bound by law but by love, and this is true spiritual freedom. Consider some other Scriptural testimonies that show us this new-found freedom experienced by the born again believer as he or she embraces the Gospel truth of salvation by Jesus Christ alone, with no contribution from the sinner as to his or her acceptance before a holy God. Here we see the true nature and evidence of the Holy Spirit's work in the spiritual realm of salvation. As Paul wrote in –

Philippians 3 – (3) For we are the circumcision, which worship God in the spirit, and rejoice in Christ Jesus, and have no confidence in the flesh.

Philippians 3 – (7) But what things were gain to me, those I counted loss for Christ. (8) Yea doubtless, and I count all things but loss for the excellency of the knowledge of Christ Jesus my Lord: for whom I have suffered the loss of all things, and do count them but dung, that I may win Christ, (9) And be found in Him, not having mine own righteousness, which is of the law, but that which is through the faith of Christ, the righteousness which is of God by faith:

This is the true nature of faith in Christ and the true nature of Godly repentance that turns away from everything but Christ and His righteousness alone for salvation. All the things Paul naturally thought gained him salvation and favor with God, all His heritage, religion, and sincerity, were all reduced to *"dung"* (refuse) in light of Christ and His righteousness. This spirit of faith in Christ and repentance of dead works and idolatry, by the grace of God in Christ Jesus through the power of the Holy Spirit, continues in the life of a born-again person unto his or her final glory. This is the subject of the next chapter.

CHAPTER

6

THE SPIRITUAL REALM OF SALVATION (PART 2)

Two vital biblical, Gospel truths that are part of the spiritual realm of salvation are:

**I. THE PRESERVATION OF THE SAVED
BY GOD'S GRACE IN CHRIST,**
and
**II. THE PERSEVERANCE OF THE SAVED
BY GOD'S GRACE IN CHRIST.**

The reason we need to consider these truths is not only because they are vital parts of the spiritual realm of salvation in the work of the Holy Spirit within God's people, but also because of some of the greatest errors and misunderstandings among people today on the subject of salvation. I stated these things in the introduction to this whole series of studies, but they bear repeating here. So many people today think of salvation as merely a one-time event in a person's life, something that took place in the past when that person, as many say, "made a decision for Christ," or "got baptized," or "joined the church." This has led many people to think wrongly that salvation is a one-time event – often something that happened in childhood or youth when they "gave their heart to Jesus." This is not a biblical way of understanding salvation.

As I have already pointed out, in the New Testament the verb "to save" appears virtually in every possible tense of the Greek language. We have seen how there is a sense in which those who are saved have always been saved from before the world began in the mind and purpose of God. There is a sense in which they were saved when Christ died on the cross as their Substitute and Surety. There is a sense in which they were saved when born again by the Holy Spirit and brought to believe in the Lord Jesus Christ and call upon His name. The subject of this chapter is the present tense of salvation wherein all who are saved by God's grace are BEING SAVED as they are preserved by God's power and grace and by which they persevere (continue) in the faith unto final glory. Salvation is more than merely a one-time event in a person's life. In the spiritual realm of salvation, having been born again by the Holy Spirit, the saved sinner continues in the life of salvation by the grace and power of God in the Lord Jesus Christ.

Biblical salvation involves a lifetime of trusting, resting in, and following the Lord Jesus Christ for all salvation. A common objection to this is, "What about the thief on the cross? He was converted at his death." This is true, but it is clear from the Bible that whatever life here on earth he had left, he lived it looking to Jesus Christ as the Author and Finisher of his faith *(Hebrews 12:2)*. This is true of all born-again persons, whether they are converted by the Holy Spirit early in life, like Timothy, or even at their death, like the thief on the cross. Another common objection is the one the Apostle Paul anticipated in *Romans 6* after having made clear that all of salvation is conditioned, not on the saved sinner, nor on the works of sinners, but solely upon the Lord Jesus Christ. It is all by the righteousness of God in Christ alone. Paul stated the objection this way –

Romans 6 – (1) What shall we say then? Shall we continue in sin, that grace may abound?

Unbelievers today state this same objection to the eternal security of the saved by accusing us of saying that a person can be a Christian but live a life of sin and disobedience without repentance and Godly sorrow over sin. Many object, "You're saying it doesn't matter how we live." That is not what I am saying, and it is not what the Bible teaches. Let's consider first –

I. THE PRESERVATION OF THE SAVED

There are seven Gospel truths to be considered under this heading –

(1) All who are truly saved by God's grace in Jesus Christ are preserved unto final glorification by the power and grace of God in Christ Jesus. Truly saved people can never be condemned or lost again. I know this flies in the face of much religion today that comes in the name of Christianity while claiming to believe that a sinner can be saved and then lost either by leaving the Gospel or by turning back to a life of unbelief and/or immorality. Many believe in what is called a conditional preservation of the saints, or commonly called "conditional security." This is the idea that believers are kept safe by God in their saving relationship with Him upon the condition of a persevering (continuing) faith in Christ and/or life of obedience and good works. Preservation, or security, to them, therefore, is not totally by God's grace and power but by the believer continuing to be better than before. This is nothing more than false Christianity, legalism, and a false gospel. The reason so many believe salvation can be lost is because they believe salvation can be gained and/or maintained by some condition(s) sinners meet, at least in some way, at some stage, to some degree. It would stand to reason that if I do something to gain my salvation, then I could do something to lose it, but that is salvation by works, not by grace. The Bible teaches us that sinners are saved by grace, kept (preserved) by grace, and ultimately brought to final glory in heaven by grace.

(2) The reality of our sin even after the new birth proves that we cannot keep or preserve ourselves in the faith. Those who believe that final glory is conditioned upon the believer's continuance in the faith do not know the reality of their own sin. We have spoken much of the reality of our sin before we are converted, that we have been ruined with Adam in the fall, that we are born spiritually dead in trespasses and sin, and that we cannot be saved by our best efforts to do anything pleasing unto God, not even our faith. But what about after we are converted? The Apostle Paul described it in **Romans 7:14-25** showing that due to the remaining corruption, influence, and contamination of sinful flesh, while on this earth a true believer can never attain his desired goal of being perfectly conformed to Jesus Christ in character and conduct. There is a spiritual warfare going on within every born-again person, so much so that, as Paul states, even as sinners saved by grace, nothing we do can be counted as measuring up to the standard of perfect righteousness. We must cry with the apostle –

Romans 7 – (22) For I delight in the law of God after the inward man: (23) But I see another law in my members, warring against the law of my mind, and bringing me into captivity to the law of sin which is in my members. (24) O wretched man that I am! who shall deliver me from the body of this death? (25) I thank God through Jesus Christ our Lord. So then with the mind I myself serve the law of God; but with the flesh the law of sin.

The point of this is that not only can we not save ourselves, but we cannot keep ourselves in the faith. Our continuation and final glory in heaven is the work of God's power, goodness, and grace in Christ, not our own. We must say with the psalmist that if at any time in our Christian lives God would mark our iniquities (sins), we would not and could not stand the test – *"If Thou, LORD, shouldest mark iniquities, O Lord, who shall stand?" (Psalm 130:3).*

(3) The power of Christ Himself is the power of preservation unto glory for His people. The Lord Jesus Christ said –

John 6 – (37) All that the Father giveth Me shall come to Me; and him that cometh to Me I will in no wise cast out. (38) For I came down from heaven, not to do Mine own will, but the will of Him that sent Me.

(39) And this is the Father's will which hath sent Me, that of all which He hath given Me I should lose nothing, but should raise it up again at the last day. (40) And this is the will of Him that sent Me, that every one which seeth the Son, and believeth on Him, may have everlasting life: and I will raise him up at the last day.

John 10 – (27) My sheep hear My voice, and I know them, and they follow Me: (28) And I give unto them eternal life; and THEY SHALL NEVER PERISH, neither shall any man pluck them out of My hand. (29) My Father, which gave them Me, is greater than all; and no man is able to pluck them out of My Father's hand. (30) I and my Father are one.

The Apostle Paul wrote –

Romans 8 – (31) What shall we then say to these things? If God be for us, who can be against us? (32) He that spared not His own Son, but delivered Him up for us all, how shall He not with Him also freely give us all things? (33) Who shall lay any thing to the charge of God's elect? It is God that justifies. (34) Who is he that comdemns? It is Christ that died, yes rather, that is risen again, who is even at the right hand of God, who also makes intercession for us. (35) Who shall separate us from the love of Christ? shall tribulation, or distress, or persecution, or famine, or nakedness, or peril, or sword? (36) As it is written, For your sake we are killed all the day long; we are accounted as sheep for the slaughter. (37) No, in all these things we are more than conquerors through Him that loved us. (38) For I am persuaded, that neither death, nor life, nor angels, nor principalities, nor powers, nor things present, nor things to come, (39) Nor height, nor depth, nor any other creature, shall be able to separate us from the love of God, which is in Christ Jesus our Lord.

Philippians 1 – (6) Being confident of this very thing, that he which hath begun a good work in you will perform it until the day of Jesus Christ:

Philippians 2 – (12) Wherefore, my beloved, as ye have always obeyed, not as in my presence only, but now much more in my absence, work out your own salvation with fear and trembling. (13) For it is God which worketh in you both to will and to do of His good pleasure.

Hebrews 13 – (20) Now the God of peace, that brought again from the dead our Lord Jesus, that great Shepherd of the sheep, through the blood of the everlasting covenant, (21) Make you perfect in every good work to do His will, working in you that which is wellpleasing in His sight, through Jesus Christ; to whom be glory for ever and ever. Amen.

We do not doubt God's ability, and salvation is by HIS ability, not ours –

2 Timothy – (12) For the which cause I also suffer these things: nevertheless I am not ashamed: for I know whom I have believed, and am persuaded that he is able to keep that which I have committed unto him against that day.

Hebrews 7 – (24) But this man, because He continueth ever, hath an unchangeable priesthood. (25) Wherefore He is able also to save them to the uttermost that come unto God by Him, seeing He ever liveth to make intercession for them.

Jude – (24) Now unto Him that is able to keep you from falling, and to present you faultless before the presence of His glory with exceeding joy, (25) To the only wise God our Saviour, be glory and majesty, dominion and power, both now and ever. Amen.

Hebrews 13 – (5) Let your conversation be without covetousness; and be content with such things as ye have: for He hath said, I will never leave thee, nor forsake thee.

Jeremiah 31 – (34) for I will forgive their iniquity, and I will remember their sin no more.

(4) **The nature and terms of the everlasting covenant of grace, of which Jesus Christ is Surety, proves the preservation of all who are truly saved.** We see this taught in the Old Testament prophecies of the New Covenant. The New Covenant is the establishment in time of all the conditions of the everlasting covenant of grace made before time, meaning from eternity past. Christ was set up in the everlasting covenant of grace to be the Surety of that covenant. The Bible tells us that all of its conditions were placed upon Him alone –

Isaiah 9 – (6) For unto us a child is born, unto us a son is given: and the government shall be upon His shoulder: and His name shall be called Wonderful, Counsellor, The mighty God, The everlasting Father, The Prince of Peace. (7) Of the increase of His government and peace there shall be no end, upon the throne of David, and upon His kingdom, to order it, and to establish it with judgment and with justice from henceforth even for ever. The zeal of the LORD of hosts will perform this.

When Isaiah preached *"the government shall be upon His shoulder,"* the meaning is that the establishment, growth, salvation, prosperity, and victory of the whole church of God would be upon Jesus Christ to accomplish it. It was and is all conditioned on Christ as Surety. Jeremiah prophesied of this and made a distinct contrast between the Old Covenant and the New Covenant –

Jeremiah 31 – (31) Behold, the days come, saith the LORD, that I will make a new covenant with the house of Israel, and with the house of Judah: (32) Not according to the covenant that I made with their fathers in the day that I took them by the hand to bring them out of the land of Egypt; which My covenant they brake, although I was an husband unto them, saith the LORD: (33) But this shall be the covenant that I will make with the house of Israel; After those days, saith the LORD, I will put my law in their inward parts, and write it in their hearts; and will be their God, and they shall be my people. (34) And they shall teach no more every man his neighbour, and every man his brother, saying, Know the LORD: for they shall all know Me, from the least of them unto the greatest of them, saith the LORD: for I will forgive their iniquity, and I will remember their sin no more.

Jeremiah 32 – (40) And I will make an everlasting covenant with them, that I will not turn away from them, to do them good; but I will put My fear in their hearts, that they shall not depart from Me.

So true believers are part of an everlasting covenant of grace all conditioned on Christ Who is the Surety of the covenant. We saw this in the eternal realm of salvation as believers are chosen in Christ, the elect of God, from the very beginning. We saw this in the legal realm of salvation as believers were redeemed by Christ, the Surety of the covenant, Who fulfilled all conditions of the covenant in righteousness to secure the salvation of His people and to purchase for them the gift of eternal life and faith. We see this in the spiritual realm of salvation as God's people are brought into this covenant experientially as they are born again by the Holy Spirit and brought to believe in the Lord Jesus Christ. This is how David could express personally and confidently at his death the assurance of salvation and glory –

2 Samuel 23 – (5) Although my house be not so with God; yet He hath made with me an everlasting covenant, ordered in all things, and sure: for this is all my salvation, and all my desire, although He make it not to grow.

As the Lord Jesus Christ is the *"Surety of a better testament"* (covenant) *(Hebrews 7:22), "wherefore He is able also to save them to the uttermost that come unto God by Him, seeing He ever liveth to make intercession for them." (Heb. 7:25)* True believers are not self-saved people. They are the creation of God in Christ, the fruit of what Christ accomplished on Calvary.

(5) **True believers cannot be charged with sin.** Those who are truly saved, truly in Christ, cannot be charged with sin because Christ has already been charged, found guilty, and taken the punishment of all those sins as their Substitute –

2 Corinthians 5 – (21) For He [God the Father] *hath made Him* [God the Son incarnate] *to be sin for us,* [Christ] *Who knew no sin; that we might be made the righteousness of God in Him.*

This is the great legal exchange that took place on the cross when Jesus Christ gave His own life *"a ransom for many" (Matt. 20:28),* all whom the Father had given Him before the foundation of the world. Having their sins charged to Him, they cannot be justly charged with them ever again –

Romans 4 – (6) Even as David also describeth the blessedness of the man, unto whom God imputeth righteousness without works, (7) Saying, Blessed are they whose iniquities are forgiven, and whose sins are covered. (8) Blessed is the man to whom the Lord will not impute sin.

Romans 8 – (33) Who shall lay any thing to the charge of God's elect? It is God that justifieth. (34) Who is he that condemneth? It is Christ that died, yea rather, that is risen again, who is even at the right hand of God, who also maketh intercession for us.

This does not mean that while on this earth we who are true believers are not still sinners. Though there is much sin in us and done by us, yet God cannot and will not charge us with sin or condemn us for it. The Lord Jesus Christ came into the world to destroy, purge, remove, and take away all the sins of His people, and He has done it. All the sins of God's elect were laid upon Christ. He bore them in His own body on the tree, endured and satisfied the wrath of God for them and bore them away. The Son of God redeemed His people from the curse of the law, made an end of their sins, and justified and sanctified them by His blood. God Almighty has, through the effectual, redemptive work of Christ, so thoroughly blotted out the sins of His elect that He does not hold them against them.

(6) The righteousness by which saved sinners are justified is the imputed righteousness of Christ, God the Son incarnate. The righteousness of God, which is by Jesus Christ, is a perfect, eternal, unchangeable righteousness which God will never take away. It cannot be removed or even contaminated with sin. It is the righteousness of God in Christ as it is the merit of Christ, the Godman, and His work of obedience unto death. Christ is the Advocate of His people, and He continually intercedes on their behalf –

Romans 8 – (33) Who shall lay any thing to the charge of God's elect? It is God that justifieth. (34) Who is he that condemneth? It is Christ that died, yea rather, that is risen again, Who is even at the right hand of God, Who also maketh intercession for us.

Hebrews 7 – (25) Wherefore He is able also to save them to the uttermost that come unto God by Him, seeing He ever liveth to make intercession for them.

1 John 2 – (1) My little children, these things write I unto you, that ye sin not. And if any man sin, we have an advocate with the Father, Jesus Christ the righteous: (2) And He is the propitiation for our sins: and not for ours only, but also for the sins of the whole world.

True believers cannot lose salvation because Christ never quits pleading the merits of His righteousness on their behalf.

(7) True believers can never totally leave and forsake Christ. This brings us to the second major point of this lesson –

II. THE PERSEVERANCE OF THE SAVED BY GOD'S GRACE IN CHRIST

Recall what we read in the prophecy of Jeremiah –

Jeremiah 32 – (40) And I will make an everlasting covenant with them, that I will not turn away from them, to do them good; but I will put My fear in their hearts, that THEY SHALL NOT DEPART FROM ME.

Israel under the Old Covenant departed from the Lord. The covenant under which they lived for nearly 1500 years was a conditional covenant towards that nation. And because that nation, like all men by nature, was made up of sinful people, that covenant of law was destined to be broken as the people were destined to fail to meet its conditions. Why was it given?

Romans 5 – (20) Moreover the law entered, that the offence might abound. But where sin abounded, grace did much more abound: (21) That as sin hath reigned unto death, even so might grace reign through righteousness unto eternal life by Jesus Christ our Lord.

The Old Covenant law was given to Israel to show them their sinfulness and their need of salvation by God's grace in Jesus Christ. That need cannot be met by a covenant of law. It can only be satisfied in the covenant of grace. This covenant is kept by the Lord Jesus Christ Who saves His people and keeps them from departing and falling away. True believers will persevere (continue) in the faith of Jesus Christ. They will never totally quit believing and following Christ. They can get side-tracked and lose sight of reality for a while, but they cannot totally apostatize (fall away) from the faith. Why? As stated, because God by His grace and power in the Lord Jesus Christ preserves them, but He does it by means. What are these means? Let's consider God's means of preservation by which the true people of God persevere:

(1) The continual indwelling presence and power of God the Holy Spirit –

John 14 – (16) And I will pray the Father, and He shall give you another Comforter, that He may abide with you for ever; (17) Even the Spirit of truth; whom the world cannot receive, because it seeth Him not, neither knoweth Him: but ye know Him; for He dwelleth with you, and shall be in you.

2 Corinthians 1 – (20) For all the promises of God in Him are yea, and in Him Amen, unto the glory of God by us. (21) Now He which stablisheth us with you in Christ, and hath anointed us, is God; (22)

Who hath also sealed us, and given the earnest of the Spirit in our hearts.

Ephesians 1 – (10) That in the dispensation of the fulness of times He might gather together in one all things in Christ, both which are in heaven, and which are on earth; even in Him: (11) In Whom also we have obtained an inheritance, being predestinated according to the purpose of Him who worketh all things after the counsel of His own will: (12) That we should be to the praise of His glory, who first trusted in Christ. (13) In whom ye also trusted, after that ye heard the word of truth, the gospel of your salvation: in Whom also after that ye believed, ye were sealed with that holy Spirit of promise, (14) Which is the earnest of our inheritance until the redemption of the purchased possession, unto the praise of His glory.

This is the reality of Christ Himself dwelling within His people BY HIS SPIRIT and BY HIS WORD.

(2) The new life, new heart, new spirit given and imparted whereby the word of God is written on the hearts of His people so that they cannot totally leave and forsake Christ –

1 John 2 – (18) Little children, it is the last time: and as ye have heard that antichrist shall come, even now are there many antichrists; whereby we know that it is the last time. (19) They went out from us, but they were not of us; for if they had been of us, they would no doubt have continued with us: but they went out, that they might be made manifest that they were not all of us. (20) But ye have an unction from the Holy One, and ye know all things.

1 John 2 – (24) Let that therefore abide in you, which ye have heard from the beginning. If that which ye have heard from the beginning shall remain in you, ye also shall continue in the Son, and in the Father. (25) And this is the promise that he hath promised us, even eternal life. (26) These things have I written unto you concerning them that seduce you. (27) But the anointing which ye have received of Him abideth in you, and ye need not that any man teach you: but as the same anointing teacheth you of all things, and is truth, and is no lie, and even as it hath taught you, ye shall abide in Him.

One of the most difficult and misunderstood passages of Scripture in the Bible is found in *1 John 3*. Read the following portion of this chapter keeping in mind that the apostle is speaking of (1) those who are false children of God, false professors, who had fallen away from the faith revealing they were never saved, and (2) true children of God, true believers, who could not and would not fall away but who would continue by the grace of God to believe, follow, and cling to Christ. I have added some commentary to help you in reading and understanding–

1 John 3 – (4) Whosoever committeth sin transgresseth also the law: for sin is the transgression of the law. (5) And ye know that He [Jesus Christ] *was manifested to take away our sins; and in Him is no sin.* [In Christ personally there is no sin, but the point here is that as believers are considered and stand in Him as their Subsitute and Surety, they have no sin charged to them.] *(6) Whosoever abideth in Him sinneth not: whosoever sinneth hath not seen Him, neither known Him.* [All who continue in Christ, clinging by faith to Him, do not sin in the sense they cannot leave Him. All who leave Christ have never seen Him with the eye of faith and have never known Him savingly. – cf. 1 John 2:18-19] *(7) Little children, let no man deceive you: he that doeth righteousness is righteous, even as He is righteous. (8) He that committeth sin is of the devil; for the devil sinneth from the beginning. For this purpose the Son of God was manifested, that He might destroy the works of the devil. (9) Whosoever is born of God doth not commit sin;* [Those born of God do not leave Christ] *FOR HIS SEED* [Christ's offspring, God's true children] *REMAINETH IN HIM:* [continue with Christ] *and he cannot sin,* [A true child of God cannot totally forsake or leave Christ.] *because he is born of God.* [Because they are born again by the Spirit.]

Having been born of God by the Holy Spirit, true believers can never be lost again. They can never totally forsake the Lord Jesus Christ unto apostasy (damnation). As stated before, they are all kept, preserved, by the grace, power, and goodness of Almighty God through the Lord Jesus Christ Who is their salvation. They will all be preserved unto final glory which is the subject of the next chapter.

C H A P T E R

7

THE GLORIFIED REALM OF SALVATION (PART 1)

The glorified realm of salvation is the final state of all those saved by the grace of God in Christ Jesus in the completion and consummation of all things unto perfection. This is when the whole church of the Lord Jesus Christ, each individual member of His body, will be perfectly conformed to His image. Believers, who are already sinlessly perfect judicially in Christ, will be sinlessly perfect in themselves with no presence, influence, or contamination of sin in their lives. This aspect of salvation is future for all the saints of the Lord. It will take place at the second coming of Christ when He returns to gather His people unto Himself and to judge the world in righteousness, thus, glorifying His church and subduing all His enemies unto condemnation. In the *Book of Romans*, the Apostle Paul instructs the people of God, true believers, to be obedient citizens while living in the world. He wrote –

Romans 13 – (11) And that, knowing the time, that now it is high time to awake out of sleep: for now is our salvation nearer than when we believed.

When Paul wrote, *"our salvation is nearer than when we believed,"* he meant that their complete deliverance from this world, from the presence, influence, and contamination of the remaining sin of the flesh, i.e. their final glorification in the new heavens and the new earth, was nearer in time than when they first came to believe in the Lord Jesus Christ. Paul also expressed the future tense of salvation in –

Romans 7 – (24) O wretched man that I am! who shall deliver me from the body of this death?

Here we see that the believer's final glory is due to the sovereign grace, mercy, and power of God in the Lord Jesus Christ and not due to the believer's faith, works, and/or perseverance. Because of the grace of God in Christ, true believers will bear the fruit of good works, obedience, and perseverance in the faith, not so as to earn, merit, or attain final glory, but because of God's grace in Christ Jesus Who has earned, merited, and attained final glory for His people. Just as the spiritual realm of salvation is the fruit of Christ's death on the cross, the glorified realm of salvation is also the fruit of His death, His righteousness imputed. To understand something of the glorified realm of salvation, we must first understand what every true believer can say of himself according to God's Word. This knowledge comes as believers are taught of God and convinced by the Holy Spirit.

(1) Every true believer knows he or she has been fully and finally saved from the penalty of sin.

Romans 8 – (1) There is therefore now no condemnation to them which are in Christ Jesus, who walk not after the flesh, but after the Spirit.

1 John 4 – (17) Herein is our love made perfect, that we may have boldness in the day of judgment: because as He is, so are we in this world.

Every true believer has the assurance of being justified before God in Christ. The true child of God has been fully cleansed from all sin by the blood of Christ and stands before God clothed in Christ's righteousness imputed so much so that he can say with confidence, "As Christ is, so am I in this world." This speaks only of the believer's judicial standing before God in the Lord Jesus Christ. This is the believer's reality and desire –

Philippians 3 – (7) But what things were gain to me, those I counted loss for Christ. (8) Yea doubtless, and I count all things but loss for the excellency of the knowledge of Christ Jesus my Lord: for Whom I have suffered the loss of all things, and do count them but dung, that I may win Christ, (9) And be found in Him, not having mine own righteousness, which is of the law, but that which is through the faith of Christ, the righteousness which is of God by faith:

I stated this in the last chapter, and it bears repeating – Though there is much sin in us and done by us, yet God cannot and will not charge us with sin or condemn us for it. The Lord Jesus Christ came into the world to destroy, purge, remove, and take away all the sins of His people, and He has done it.

(2) Every true believer has been fully and finally saved from the power of sin in the sense of being delivered from spiritual death, darkness, and unbelief.

Colossians 1 – (12) Giving thanks unto the Father, which hath made us meet to be partakers of the inheritance of the saints in light: (13) Who hath delivered us from the power of darkness, and hath translated us into the kingdom of His dear Son:

While here on this earth true believers have not been delivered from the power of sin as it pertains to the remaining influence and contamination of the flesh. This is why all believers are constantly engaged in spiritual warfare – the warfare of the Spirit against the flesh –

Galataians 5 – (16) This I say then, Walk in the Spirit, and ye shall not fulfil the lust of the flesh. (17) For the flesh lusteth against the Spirit, and the Spirit against the flesh: and these are contrary the one to the other: so that ye cannot do the things that ye would.

Remaining sin within true believers is still powerful enough to keep them from fulfilling their God-given desire to be perfectly conformed to Jesus Christ in character, attitude, and conduct. It can be said, however, that they are no longer spiritually dead as they have been quickened, made alive, by the Holy Spirit. They are no longer deceived by Satan so as to be in the darkness of sin that keeps them from seeing the glory of God in Christ. They are no longer in a state of unbelief as they have been brought by the Spirit to faith in Christ and true repentance. Though they still have unbelief within them, they are not in a state of unbelief. True believers, while still on this earth, have the flesh still within them and must fight against the flesh, but, as the Apostle Paul wrote –

Romans 8 – (9) But ye are not in the flesh, but in the Spirit, if so be that the Spirit of God dwell in you. Now if any man have not the Spirit of Christ, he is none of His.

(3) While in this life, no true believer has been saved from the remaining presence, influence, and contamination of sin, the flesh.

Philippians 3 – (11) If by any means I might attain unto the resurrection of the dead. (12) Not as though I had already attained, either were already perfect: but I follow after, if that I may apprehend that for which also I am apprehended of Christ Jesus. (13) Brethren, I count not myself to have apprehended: but this one thing I do, forgetting those things which are behind, and reaching forth unto those things which are before, (14) I press toward the mark for the prize of the high calling of God in Christ Jesus.

If we are to understand salvation as revealed in the Bible, we who are saved must maintain the distinction of what we are judicially in Christ (righteous and perfect based on the merits of His obedience unto death imputed to us) and what we are spiritually within ourselves (born-again, quickened, converted with new hearts, new spirits, but still influenced and contaminated with sin in all that we think, say, and do). Paul expressed this –

Romans 7 – (18) For I know that in me (that is, in my flesh,) dwelleth no good thing: for to will is present with me; but how to perform that which is good I find not. (19) For the good that I would I do not: but the evil which I would not, that I do.

Paul, like David of old, had a God-given desire to be perfect within himself, but he realized that he had not yet arrived to that state. Consider once again the words of David who was confident of being already perfect in Christ by imputation –

Romans 4 – (6) Even as David also describeth the blessedness of the man, unto whom God imputeth righteousness without works, (7) Saying, Blessed are they whose iniquities are forgiven, and whose sins are covered. (8) Blessed is the man to whom the Lord will not impute sin.

But David also knew that while he was yet in this life, he had no perfection of righteousness within himself –

Psalm 17 – (15) As for me, I will behold Thy face in righteousness: I shall be satisfied, when I awake, with Thy likeness.

We must understand that this is no diminishing of, insult to, or affront against the blessed, powerful, and perfect work of the Holy Spirit in God's people. What God the Holy Spirit does within God's people is a perfect work and a miraculous change within them. But as that work is expressed through them as sinners saved by grace, through their minds, affections, and wills, it is contaminated by the remaining influences of the flesh so that they cannot do what they desire – be perfectly righteous in every way.

Some people promote the false idea that when a person is born again by the Holy Spirit, he is given a "new nature" which is holy, righteous, and perfect so that it cannot be contaminated with sin, and the "old nature" (their term for the flesh) remains nothing but sin. They present this explanation as their idea of "two natures" in a believer. They describe these "two natures" as entities, or beings, within themselves acting independent of one another as if they were two different people, one sinlessly perfect and uncontaminated, and one sinful and depraved. This is at best a confusion of reality and at worst a heresy that promotes self-righteousness. There has been much controversy and division over this issue, and much of it is merely an argument over terms. Does a believer have "two natures" within him? It depends on how one defines "two natures." For example, one definition that was given to me by one of its proponents is as follows – When a sinner is born again, the Holy Spirit "creates within him a divine nature that cannot sin and cannot be contaminated." Whatever one thinks about the term "two natures" in a believer, the Bible teaches no such doctrine as the creation of a divine nature within a believer. First of all, that which is divine cannot be created. Divinity has no beginning and no end. Secondly, the *"divine nature"* as expressed by the Apostle Peter in *2 Peter 1:4* where he wrote that believers are *"partakers of the divine nature"* is the nature of God Himself – Father, Son, and Holy Spirit. Peter is teaching that those who are born again by the Spirit, through the promises of God in the Lord Jesus Christ, are brought into fellowship with the *"divine nature"* (God Himself).

It is true that all born again persons have new hearts, new spirits, new life, new knowledge, desires, motives, and goals. Some call this "the new nature," and this is fine as long as they do not go too far as in the above example. This is divine life, or life from the divine, from God Himself, but it is not a divine nature in its essence. All born again persons are still only human. They are chosen, justified, redeemed, born-again, spiritual humans, but still human, not divine by nature. It is also true that all born again persons, while in this life, still have the remaining sin(s) of the flesh within themselves. Some call this "the old nature," and this too is fine as long as they do not go too far in going beyond what the Bible teaches on this subject. The old desires, motives, and goals have not been totally eradicated and removed. There is an inward struggle between the flesh and the Spirit within every born again person. True believers are born-again persons with new hearts, new spirits, new life within from God, even with new wills and new desires, new motives and goals. And yet all true believers know that their best efforts to love Christ and to love the brethren, their best attempts to obey the Lord, fall short of the perfection of righteousness and must be washed clean in the blood of the Lamb to be accepted by God.

(4) By the grace of God in Christ Jesus, all true believers have the security and assurance of being finally glorified and being made perfectly holy and righteous within themselves.

The glorified realm of salvation is the realm of existence into which the Lord will bring all His elect people (all who have been justified and redeemed by the blood of Christ, all who have been born again by the Holy Spirit and preserved by the grace of God) to spend eternity with Jesus Christ in the new heavens and the new earth. As stated before, it is a state of complete holiness and blessedness with no presence, influence, or contamination of sin and no hindrances of the flesh. It is immortality in the eternal bliss of perfect conformity to Christ with no hint of sin and death. It is the consummation of our personal salvation, the final stage of the application of Christ's work for us and the completion of His work in us. It is the resurrection of our bodies, not our spirits because our spirits do not die.

Philippians 3 – (20) For our conversation is in heaven; from whence also we look for the Saviour, the Lord Jesus Christ: (21) Who shall change our vile body, that it may be fashioned like unto His glorious body, according to the working whereby He is able even to subdue all things unto Himself.

This *"vile body"* of which Paul speaks is our body of humiliation, the physical body subject to pain, sorrow, sickness, weakness, and even death, all because of sin. Because of this there is within the hearts and minds of every true believer a longing to be like Christ. This glorified realm of salvation will take place in the experience of God's people when Christ returns to gather His people, His church, unto Himself, and to judge the sinful world in righteousness. The spirits of believers who die before this time are ushered directly into the presence of God to dwell with Christ. As the Lord Jesus told the thief on the cross, *"Verily I say unto thee, To day shalt thou be with Me in paradise" (Luke 23:43).*

Those who are now in the presence of the Lord have experienced the separation of body and spirit but have not yet received their glorified bodies and will not receive them until the second coming of Christ. When this happens there will be a great transformation. The Apostle Paul described it in –

1 Corinthians 15 – (51) Behold, I shew you a mystery; We shall not all sleep, but we shall all be changed, (52) In a moment, in the twinkling of an eye, at the last trump: for the trumpet shall sound, and the dead shall be raised incorruptible, and we shall be changed. (53) For this corruptible must put on incorruption, and this mortal must put on immortality.

2 Corinthians 5 – (1) For we know that if our earthly house of this tabernacle were dissolved, we have a building of God, an house not made with hands, eternal in the heavens. (2) For in this we groan, earnestly desiring to be clothed upon with our house which is from heaven: (3) If so be that being clothed we shall not be found naked. (4) For we that are in this tabernacle do groan, being burdened: not for that we would be unclothed, but clothed upon, that mortality might be swallowed up of life.

Paul spoke of the time when the spirits of believers will again be united with their new spiritual bodies so that they will no longer be without a spiritual body but able to live throughout eternity in the form God created them to enjoy. The new body is yet future, though each deceased saint is now in the presence of the Lord. Consider the three states of men as Paul described them here:

(1) Clothed in a physical body – Believers are spirits, living souls, with physical bodies;

(2) Unclothed – When we die our bodies are put in the graves and our spirits go to be with the Lord. We do not have bodies when we are in the presence of the Lord until the resurrection of the dead.

(3) Clothed again – Believers are given new spiritual bodies at the final resurrection.

This is what we who are in Christ are waiting for, and it is worth it; for it is *"an inheritance incorruptible, undefiled, which fades not away, reserved in the heavens," (1 Peter 1:4).* And we have good ground for it, a good hope through grace. It is insured and certain because of several great realities:

First, the purpose and glory of God insure the final glory of all His people as God is faithful to fulfill His promises –

Romans 8 – (29) For whom He did foreknow, He also did predestinate to be conformed to the image of His Son, that He might be the firstborn among many brethren. (30) Moreover whom He did predestinate, them He also called: and whom He called, them He also justified: and whom He justified, them He also glorified.

Philippians 1 – (6) Being confident of this very thing, that He which hath begun a good work in you will perform it until the day of Jesus Christ:

Jude (24) Now unto Him that is able to keep you from falling, and to present you faultless before the presence of His glory with exceeding joy, (25) To the only wise God our Saviour, be glory and majesty, dominion and power, both now and ever. Amen.

Secondly, the redemptive work of Jesus Christ and the righteousness He worked out and which is imputed to His people is the ground of the final glory of all His people. Just as sin results in death, righteousness results in life eternal –

John 14 – (1) Let not your heart be troubled: ye believe in God, believe also in Me. (2) In my Father's house are many mansions: if it were not so, I would have told you. I go to prepare a place for you. (3) And if I go and prepare a place for you, I will come again, and receive you unto myself; that where I am, there ye may be also.

1 Corinthians 15 – (55) O death, where is thy sting? O grave, where is thy victory? (56) The sting of death is sin; and the strength of sin is the law. (57) But thanks be to God, which giveth us the victory through our Lord Jesus Christ.

Some suggest that to be so sure of final glory is proud presumption. Yet true believers are not dissuaded by such false humility; for our hope lies not in ourselves but in One who cannot and did not fail to save His people, the Lord Jesus Christ. For those who think salvation is in some way (or to some degree) conditioned on the sinner, their assurance would be mere presumption because the Bible teaches us that salvation (or any part of it) conditioned on sinful men and women is sure to fail. The whole salvation of God's people is conditioned on Jesus Christ Who by Himself fulfilled all the conditions –

Hebrews 2 – (10) For it became Him, for Whom are all things, and by Whom are all things, in bringing many sons unto glory, to make the Captain of their salvation perfect through sufferings.

Thirdly, the resurrection of Christ Himself as the firstfruits of His people guarantees the final glory of all His people –

1 Corinthians 15 – (12) Now if Christ be preached that He rose from the dead, how say some among you that there is no resurrection of the dead? (13) But if there be no resurrection of the dead, then is Christ not risen: (14) And if Christ be not risen, then is our preaching vain, and your faith is also vain. (15) Yea, and we are found false witnesses of God; because we have testified of God that He raised up Christ: whom He raised not up, if so be that the dead rise not. (16) For if the dead rise not, then is not Christ raised: (17) And if Christ be not raised, your faith is vain; ye are yet in your sins. (18) Then they also which are fallen asleep in Christ are perished. (19) If in this life only we have hope in Christ, we are of all men most miserable. (20) But now is Christ risen from the dead, and become the firstfruits of them that slept. (21) For since by man came death, by man came also the resurrection of the dead. (22) For as in Adam all die, even so in Christ shall all be made alive. (23) But every man in his own order: Christ the firstfruits; afterward they that are Christ's at His coming.

Paul's entire argument here is based upon the inseparable union between Christ and all those for whom He lived, died, and arose. They live because He lives.

Fourthly, the work of the Holy Spirit in the new birth is the earnest of the final glory of all His people. An earnest is a down-payment that guarantees the full and final payment. Christ paid the full and final redemption price for the whole salvation of all His people. But as to their experience and enjoyment of that salvation, it does not all come at once. It comes first in the new birth, then in the preserving grace of God, and fully and finally in their glorification with Christ in the new heavens and the new earth. The gift and power of the Holy Spirit in the new birth and His ever-abiding presence in their lives as believers is the earnest of final glory –

2 Corinthians 5 – (5) Now He that hath wrought us for the selfsame thing is God, Who also hath given unto us the earnest of the Spirit.

Paul wrote in *Ephesians 1* of those who believe and how they *(13) ... were sealed with that Holy Spirit of promise, (14) Which is the earnest of our inheritance until the redemption of the purchased possession, unto the praise of His glory.*

As we have considered much Scriptural testimony on the glorified realm of salvation, I realize that there are still many questions raised by people concerning this awesome subject. For example, "What is heaven going to be like?" or "What are we who go to heaven going to be like?" We find that the Bible does not always answer such questions to the satisfaction of our curiosity. We find descriptions of heaven, the new earth, the New Jerusalem as having streets paved with gold, walls of precious stones. Is this literal language or symbolic? It is probably symbolic, but I know that final glory in the new heavens and the new earth will be a state of perfection for God's people – totally without the presence, influence, and contamination of sin. The Bible also tells us –

Revelation 21 – (4) And God shall wipe away all tears from their eyes; and there shall be no more death, neither sorrow, nor crying, neither shall there be any more pain: for the former things are passed away.

The Bible also says in *1 Corinthians 2 – (9) But as it is written, Eye hath not seen, nor ear heard, neither have entered into the heart of man, the things which God hath prepared for them that love Him.*

Remember, the Apostle John wrote, *it doth not yet appear what we shall be (1 John 3:2)*, but we know it will be a glorious, eternal existence, and the main thing about heaven is that believers will be forever with Christ. We do have some more information given in Scripture concerning the believer's state in final glory, and we will consider these in the next chapter.

8

THE GLORIFIED REALM
OF SALVATION
(PART 2)

As stated in the last chapter, the Bible does give us some information concerning the final glorification of the people of God in Christ Jesus. Let's consider three questions –

(1) WHO WILL BE GLORIFIED WITH CHRIST?

John 5 – (28) Marvel not at this: for the hour is coming, in the which all that are in the graves shall hear His voice, (29) And shall come forth; they that have done good, unto the resurrection of life; and they that have done evil, unto the resurrection of damnation.

Who are these ***"that have done good"*** when the Bible tells us that we are all sinners, that we all have no righteousness before God and have done no good in the sight of God? Christ explains who they are in –

John 5 – (24) Verily, verily, I say unto you, He that heareth My word, and believeth on Him that sent Me, hath everlasting life, and shall not come into condemnation; but is passed from death unto life. (25) Verily, verily, I say unto you, The hour is coming, and now is, when the dead shall hear the voice of the Son of God: and they that hear shall live. (26) For as the Father hath life in Himself; so hath He given to the Son to have life in Himself; (27) And hath given Him authority to execute judgment also, because He is the Son of man.

In the Bible, it is clearly taught that no one born of Adam is considered by God to have done good in His sight by their works, but only by being saved by the grace of God based on the goodness and righteousness of Christ, and living in a state of grace by faith in the Lord Jesus Christ. In other words, the only ones who will be resurrected unto life are those who are found IN CHRIST, having been washed in His blood and clothed in His righteousness imputed. What about Scriptures like *2 Corinthians 5:10-11* –

2 Corinthians 5 – (10) For we must all appear before the judgment seat of Christ; that every one may receive the things done in his body, according to that he hath done, whether it be good or bad. (11) Knowing therefore the terror of the Lord, we persuade men; but we are made manifest unto God; and I trust also are made manifest in your consciences.

The issue here is not what our works do for us in the sense of earning or meriting anything from God, but what our works say about us either as evidences of His grace in salvation in and by the Lord Jesus Christ, or else in condemnation based on our sins. Are our works legal efforts aimed at earning salvation which, like Cain of old, evidence unbelief of God's way of salvation in Christ, and, therefore, *"bad"* because they are fruit unto death? Or, are our works the fruit of God's love and grace in Christ, and do they evidence our faith in and love for Christ as they are the products of His power and grace and as fruit unto God? Who will be resurrected unto life? Who are those of whom it will be said they have *"done good"*? They are only those who are found to be in Christ, cleansed by His blood and clothed in His righteousness, all by the grace of God. I will pose questions two and three together because they appear in the same verse of Scripture –

1 Corinthians 15 – (35) But some man will say, How are the dead raised up? and with what body do they come?

(2) HOW ARE THE DEAD RAISED UP?

(3) WITH WHAT BODY SHALL THEY BE RAISED?

The dead are raised up through the process of physical death. I will elaborate on this more in a moment, but read the following –

1 Corinthians 15 – (36) Thou fool, that which thou sowest is not quickened, except it die:

Consider next the body with which they will be raised. Will they have the same body as before? No, but it seems that there will be an ability to recognize one another –

1 Corinthians 15 – (37) And that which thou sowest, thou sowest not that body that shall be, but bare grain, it may chance of wheat, or of some other grain: (38) But God giveth it a body as it hath pleased him, and to every seed his own body.

As an illustration, compare a tomato seed with a full grown tomato. They are the same in nature, but very different in appearance and state. Those who are resurrected unto glory will each have his/her own individual body, but the new body will be so much better and more glorious. It will be a body with only beauty and holiness with no flaws or infirmities. The glorified saint will be perfectly conformed to the perfection of the humanity of Jesus Christ. Our vile bodies become dust and mingle throughout with all the dust of the earth.

Consider, for example, how some people die in explosions and their bodies disintegrate, or those whose bodies are burned up in fires or smashed to pieces in wrecks. Some may ask, "How is God going to get ashes thrown to the wind and how is He going to find the right bones on the floor of the ocean, and how is He going to get the dust of the body of one person and distinguish it from the dust of another person?" The truth is that the resurrection of the body is not God putting us back together again, like Humpty Dumpty. The resurrection of our bodies is not the equivalent of God putting together the greatest jigsaw puzzle in the universe. The new spiritual body, which those who are resurrected with Christ will have, is not made up of the exact same particles as this vile body.

Consider the death and resurrection of Jesus Christ Himself. In His resurrection His body was some way transformed into a glorified body. The body He was born with was in every way a human body without sin. Luke wrote that He grew in wisdom, in stature, in favor with God and man *(Luke 2:52)*. But when He went into the grave, there was the burial of that old body and what came out of that grave was in some way a unique body. Some say His new body was like Adam's body before the Fall, but I do not believe Adam had a glorified body before the Fall. The glorified body will be so much better than what Adam had in the Garden. Christ's glorified body was so much more glorious that no one recognized Him until He revealed Himself, and yet when they knew who He was, they saw Him the same as He was before, with the same features but glorified. He was the same yet gloriously different. We do not know how to explain this, but we know it is true because God's Word says it is true. So even though there are a lot of unanswered questions concerning the resurrection body, we do have recorded in the Bible –

SEVEN THINGS ABOUT THE RESURRECTED BODY

(1) It will be a body without corruption – *1 Corinthians 15 – (42) So also is the resurrection of the dead. It is sown in corruption; it is raised in incorruption:*
All who have salvation are saved by an incorruptible Savior and based on His incorruptible blood and righteousness, born again by the incorruptible seed (the Word of God). They possess an incorruptible inheritance reserved in heaven for them. They are destined to be incorruptible.

(2) It will be a body of glory – *1 Corinthians 15 – (43a) It is sown in dishonour; it is raised in glory:*

The dishonor here is the contamination of sin that brings dishonor to the image of God in which we were created. Man was created to glorify God, but sin pervades our lives. All who are saved are already perfectly sinless in Christ (legally) based on His righteousness imputed, but while in these vile bodies, they still have the contamination of sin within them. In glory they will be impeccable, no corruption or even capability of being corrupted.

(3) It will be a body of strength – *1 Corinthians 15 – (43b) it is sown in weakness; it is raised in power:*
In their glorified bodies, God's people will have the power to act and think righteously. They have that power now as God the Holy Spirit has given them new life, new hearts, and new desires, but while on this earth, they do not have that power in perfection. Now the remaining presence of sinful flesh keeps them from acting and thinking righteously except as they look to Christ alone for all righteousness and seek to follow Him as motivated by grace, love, and gratitude. In glory they will be able to obey Him perfectly without any hint of sin contaminating their thoughts or their actions.

(4) It will be a spiritual body – *1 Corinthians 15 – (44) It is sown a natural body; it is raised a spiritual body. There is a natural body, and there is a spiritual body.*
This does not mean that glorified believers will be ghosts or phantoms. We really do not know a lot about this other than what we see recorded of Christ Himself in His short time here on earth after His resurrection. We know that He was able to appear without opening a door, but we also know that He ate food. The idea here is that in glory we will be fully spiritual beings without the hindrances and contamination of sinful flesh.

(5) It will be a body capable of a heavenly existence – *1 Corinthians 15 – (49) And as we have borne the image of the earthy, we shall also bear the image of the heavenly. (50) Now this I say, brethren, that flesh and blood cannot inherit the kingdom of God; neither doth corruption inherit incorruption.*

This does not mean believers will be transformed into angels and have wings and harps. It means they will be able to live in a heavenly existence, suited to spiritual, eternal life. This is in line with the spiritual nature of their new bodies.

(6) It will be a body that cannot die – *1 Corinthians 15 – (53) For this corruptible must put on incorruption, and this mortal must put on immortality. (54) So when this corruptible shall have put on incorruption, and this mortal shall have put on immortality, then shall be brought to pass the saying that is written, Death is swallowed up in victory.*

The newly resurrected and glorified body will be an immortal body without any possibility or capability of death. There will be no more death *(Revelation 21:4)*. As believers have the very righteousness of God imputed to them and the life of God imparted to them, all in and by the Lord Jesus Christ, there can be no final death for them forever.

(7) It will be a victorious body – *1 Corinthians 15 – (55) O death, where is thy sting? O grave, where is thy victory? (56) The sting of death is sin; and the strength of sin is the law. (57) But thanks be to God, which giveth us the victory through our Lord Jesus Christ.*

There will be no defeat or death, no capability of sin that brings death. It will be a complete victory over sin, Satan, the flesh, the world, and death in and by the Lord Jesus Christ. This is the glorious culmination of all things according to God's purpose as they are brought to the fullness of Jesus Christ and to the praise of the glory of God's grace in Him.

CONCLUSION

In this series of studies I have examined, not just one aspect of salvation, but the whole extent of salvation as revealed in the Bible. I want to emphasize how all the truths conveyed in this study have been supported by an abundance of Scripture. This whole book is only of value if we see that this is what God has to say about salvation in His Word. It is my prayer that all who read this book and study this subject will make it a time of serious self-examination. If you claim to be saved, ask yourself this question – "What or who really made the difference in my salvation?" Whatever or whoever made that difference in your case is your savior. If it is not Jesus Christ alone, then it cannot be Biblical salvation. For example, consider what much of so-called modern-day "Christianity" believes in light of the four realms of salvation we have studied.

(1) **The Eternal Realm of Salvation** – When many today read Bible verses that speak of "election" or the "elect" of God, how do they interpret these? In their determination to cling to controlling their own eternal destiny, they revert to the "telescope of time" view which says God looked down through the telescope of time and foresaw who would believe in Him, therefore God elected them based on their foreseen faith. But this is far from the truth of Scripture, and it denies salvation totally by the free, sovereign grace of God. It says, in essence, God saves those who are less rebellious, less stubborn, less obstinate, those who obey, believe, and cooperate. It perverts faith by making it a work done by the sinner for God rather than a work done by God for the sinner. The Apostle Paul defined election in *Romans 11:5* as *"the election of grace,"* and he wrote –

Romans 11 – (6) And if by grace, then is it no more of works: otherwise grace is no more grace. But if it be of works, then is it no more grace: otherwise work is no more work.

(2) **The Legal Realm of Salvation** – Most today consider the death of the Lord Jesus Christ and the redemption He accomplished as not really securing the salvation of any one. They claim that Christ made salvation possible if sinners would only be persuaded and do their part. They reduce the blood of Christ, His death, to no more than a blanket pardon really saving no one until a person "accepts Jesus as their personal savior." They say, "God loves everyone, and Christ died for everyone," but it means nothing unless the sinner believes and/or repents. This is a denial of the true Gospel, a denial of redemption by the grace of God in the Lord Jesus Christ. The Bible is clear that if Christ died for you, your sins are forgiven, and you will be saved – you will be born again by the Holy Spirit and brought to faith in Christ. Consider the following –

John 10 – (11) I am the good shepherd: the good shepherd giveth His life for the sheep. (27) My sheep hear My voice, and I know them, and they follow Me: (28) And I give unto them eternal life; and they shall never perish, neither shall any man pluck them out of My hand.

How do we know if Christ died for any person at all? It is only when that person is brought by God's power and grace to believe in the Lord Jesus Christ as their Savior, the Lord their righteousness.

(3) **The Spiritual Realm of Salvation** – Most today believe they are born again because of their faith. Many claim that they first respond positively to the Gospel message, believing it of their own free will, as they claim, and, as a result, they are born again. This is totally opposed to what the Bible teaches. It denies the Biblical truth that all men and women by nature are spiritually dead in trespasses and sin. It denies the Gospel of God's grace and makes faith a work of man, not a work and gift of God. Just as a physically dead person cannot breath, a spiritually dead person cannot believe. This is why the Lord Jesus said, *"Ye must be born again."* The new birth does not come because of any person's faith, goodness, or will-power. It is a sovereign act of God the Holy Spirit –

John 1 – (12) But as many as received Him, to them gave He power to become the sons of God, even to them that believe on His name: (13) Which were born, not of blood, nor of the will of the flesh, nor of the will of man, but of God.

(4) The Glorified Realm of Salvation – Most today believe their own obedience, efforts, and works insure their final glory in heaven. And many (who may or may not agree with this) claim that, at least, their works of obedience as Christians will earn them greater rewards in heaven. The Bible, however, makes it clear that ALL of salvation, including final glory in heaven, is the work of God, based on His grace in and by the Lord Jesus Christ by Whose blood alone sinners are saved and brought to heaven's glory. Christ alone earned their reward *(Ephesians 1:3)*. As sinners, and even as sinner's saved by grace, believers do not earn blessings or positions in heaven from God. It is all of grace in Christ Jesus –

Jude – (24) Now unto Him that is able to keep you from falling, and to present you faultless before the presence of His glory with exceeding joy, (25) To the only wise God our Saviour, be glory and majesty, dominion and power, both now and ever. Amen.

God has arranged it so that in the salvation of sinners He alone will be glorified as the Lord Jesus Christ alone is exalted to the place of preeminence. Sinners saved by grace have nothing in which to boast except Jesus Christ and Him crucified *(Galatians 6:14; Philippians 3:3)*. I will conclude this whole study by a quotation from the Bible that summarizes the ultimate purpose of all things, especially in the salvation of sinners by Jesus Christ –

1 Corinthians 1 – (29) That no flesh should glory in His presence. (30) But of Him are ye in Christ Jesus, Who of God is made unto us wisdom, and righteousness, and sanctification, and redemption: (31) That, according as it is written, He that glorieth, let Him glory in the Lord.

THE END